Quick Reference Guide™

Graphic Design

for Desktop Publishing

J. Schwartzman

14 East 38 St New York, NY 10016

First Dictation Disc Printing
Catalog No. GD-2

ISBN: 1-56243-204-4

10   9   8   7   6   5   4   3

Printed in the United States of America

Introduction

If you're reading this book, chances are you already know one of the secrets of desktop publishing: all the computer manuals in the world won't help you make a better looking page.

There's only one way to do that, and that's by applying the visual guidelines developed over centuries by graphic artists, type designers, and printers. Though the tools may have changed — we use computers instead of hand-set type — the principles have stayed the same.

That's where *Graphic Design for Desktop Publishing* comes in. One of the best ways to learn the principles of graphic design is to learn the terms and then apply them. It's easy to do; you probably already know what many of the words in this book mean. But now, each time you look up a word, you get a design tip; not just a definition, but a suggestion that will help you make immediate improvements to your work. And each definition comes with examples so you can fully understand the term.

In the second part of the book, you will find many examples of designs you can follow. Use them either as a basis for your own work, as a source for ideas, or as a way to practice your graphic design skills.

Our goal is to help you take the guess work out of design, and make better and easier choices as you pursue desktop publishing. You'll see the difference a good basis in graphic design can make; and everyone else will see it too, as you start to turn out professional documents and publications.

Continued

Credits

I would like to gratefully acknowledge the following people for their help in assembling the information included in this book. Their respect for accuracy and quality mas made a difference.

Thank you to Ron Day of Sterling Color in New York City for his extensive technical assistance.

I would like to thank DDC authors, Iris Blanc, Margaret Brown, and Don Gosselin for their fine books on the desktop publishing powers of the PC.

Many thanks to Kathy Berkemeyer and Rebecca Fiala for their skilled and precise editing. Also, thanks to Sherri Nuti for her creative contribution and production help, along with Jay Harris and Nazneen Qazi.

Finally, I would like to acknowledge publishers Don Gosselin, Peter McCarthy and John Visaggi, for their insights into today's desktop publishers.

Please Note

All of the organizations, companies and individuals used in the many design examples included in this book are fictional. Any resemblance to a real company or person is purely accidental, and should it happen, we invite the coincidentally named parties to enjoy and use the logo that bears their name.

Continued

Contents

Continued

Study Tracks

For those who would like to use this book as more than a reference guide, you can pursue your study of graphic design by looking up sets of related words.

The study tracks suggested below will give you insight into three particular aspects of graphic communication — printing, typography, and graphic design.

Look up the word suggested in each track, in the order presented here, to get an overview of the subject. Remember that all three of these fields are tremendously rich and complex in their own right; we offer only an introduction. If you are truly interested in any of these areas, there are hundreds of fine texts on each of these fascinating subjects.

PRINTING

GRAPHIC DESIGN

TYPOGRAPHY

Start with the Basics

To get the most out of this book, take time to familiarize yourself with these basic terms. They are all referred to in more depth elsewhere in the book, but by reviewing them now, you will get a headstart on understanding all the material that follows.

TYPE BASICS

Below is an illustration showing the parts of a letter. You will see these terms used again throughout the book. They are the standard terms that apply to all typefaces, and are regularly used to talk about type.

Continued

COMPUTER BASICS

Some of the basic computer terms used in this book are listed below.

CPU: Central processing unit; your computer.

Hard drive: The device where your computer stores data. Hard drives, along with floppy disks and other storage media, all retain your data whether your computer is turned on or off.

Monitor: Your computer screen.

Platform: The hardware environment in which your operating system is working. PC, Mac, Sun, and Unix are examples of different platforms.

Program: Your application or software

Mouse: An input device that lets users select information by clicking and dragging.

Printer: An output device that takes your file and prints it out to paper or film.

RAM: Short for random access memory. A temporary storage space for data and programs. Ram is only active when your computer is turned on.

MEASURING BASICS

In typesetting and graphic design, type is measured in *points*. There are 72 points in an inch.

The next larger measurement is *picas*. There are six picas in an inch. Picas are generally used for longer measurements such as the width of a line or the length of a column.

An *em* or *em quad* is the width of a letter "M" within a particular typeface and a particular size of type. For example, in six point type, an em is six points; in twelve point type, an em is twelve points. An *en* is half an em. Long dashes are called em dashes. Short dashes are called *en dashes*.

Continued

Accent Marks

äbç

Accent marks are added to letters in order to indicate correct pronunciation.

Accent marks are commonly used in French, Spanish, Italian and German; in English, they are rarely used. Accent marks are also called *diacriticals*.

Most programs let you apply accent marks using a special character, symbol font, or certain keystroke combinations.

DEMONSTRATION

These are some common accent marks you may see:

é	Grave	café; resumé
è	Acute	lumière; Molière
ç	Cedilla	façon
â	Circumflex	châteaux; fête
ä	Umlaut	übergeben; für
ñ	Tilde	mañana; piñata

DESIGN TIPS

- If you are using a foreign word in your text, an accented name, or an English word that is accented, it is good form to include the accent mark.

- Foreign words and phrases should also be italicized.

Alignment

Alignment refers to the way lines of text are arranged relative to the edges of a block of copy.

There are four kinds of alignment in most desktop publishing programs: justified, left, right and center.

If a block of copy is *justified,* all lines of text begin at the same point on the left and end at the same point on the right. *Left alignment* means all text lines up on the left and remains uneven or ragged on the right. *Right alignment* means all text lines up on the right and remains uneven or ragged on the left. *Centered alignment* means lines of text are aligned on their center point.

You may also hear the the terms *flush left* and *flush right* used when talking about alignment. These are the traditional typesetting terms for left and right alignment. Another word for alignment is *justification.*

Alignment, in a general sense, refers to the relationship between any set of items; you can align tabs, graphics, baselines and other items within a document.

Note that a handful of programs — WordPerfect® being the most common — use the terms *left justified* and *right justified* to mean flush left and flush right.

DEMONSTRATION

These are examples of different kinds of alignment:

Justified:

Printers are educated in the belief, that when men differ in opinion, both sides ought equally to have the advantage of being heard by the publick; and that when truth and error have fair play, the former is always an overmatch for the latter.

Benjamin Franklin

Left alignment (or flush left):

Printers are educated in the belief, that when men differ in opinion, both sides ought equally to have the advantage of being heard by the publick; and that when truth and error have fair play, the former is always an overmatch for the latter.

Benjamin Franklin

Right alignment (or flush right):

Printers are educated in the belief, that when men differ in opinion, both sides ought equally to have the advantage of being heard by the publick; and that when truth and error have fair play, the former is always an over-match for the latter.

Benjamin Franklin

Center:

Printers are educated in the belief, that when men differ in opinion, both sides ought equally to have the advantage of being heard by the publick; and that when truth and error have fair play, the former is always an overmatch for the latter.

Benjamin Franklin

DESIGN TIPS

- Justified type will give your page a cleaner, more organized look. It is by far the most common way of setting type for newspapers and books. Type that is left aligned adds interest and variety, and is often easier to read.

Continued

ALIGNMENT

- When you justify text, make sure your line length is long enough to allow for at least five or six words per line, otherwise, you may get awkward spaces between words:

> **The   Alamo   Boot**
> **Company produces the**
> **finest quality footwear.**
> **Every pair of Alamo boots**
> **is   hand-crafted   with**
> **superior skill.**

This kind of uneven spacing is not only unattractive, it's difficult to read. In this case, it would be better to set your copy flush left:

> **The Alamo Boot**
> **Company produces the**
> **finest quality footwear.**
> **Every pair of Alamo**
> **boots is hand-crafted**
> **with superior skill.**

- Centered copy is hard to read in long passages. It's more appropriate for short blocks of information such as invitations, headlines or short advertising copy:

Alamo Boots: Designed for
the Great Outdoors

or:

Sanchez & Needleman
Tax Preparers
have moved.
Please visit us
at our new offices.

Baseline

A baseline is an imaginary horizontal line upon which type rests.

You can align blocks of text that are side-by-side, by aligning their baselines. For example, if you have two columns on a page, the baseline of the first line of each column should align across both columns.

DEMONSTRATION

If you were to draw a line under a row of letters, that would be the baseline:

Pleased to meet you.

DESIGN TIPS

• Use baselines to align text that appears side-by-side:

Neighborhood News: Helping Hand Literacy Volunteers celebrate their fifth year of helping youngsters and grown-ups develop their reading skills.

Join them for an anniversary celebration this Thursday night at the Alta Mira Youth Center.

Bitmap

A bitmap is a type of graphic file. In a bitmap, a graphic or font is represented pixel-by-pixel, mapped to a grid.

In the case of a screen bitmap, the grid corresponds to the pixels on a monitor. In a bitmap, every pixel is either black or white, thus defining the image.

Bitmaps often lack detail because there is a limited amount of information that can be contained in the file.

DEMONSTRATION

Below is an example of a bitmap:

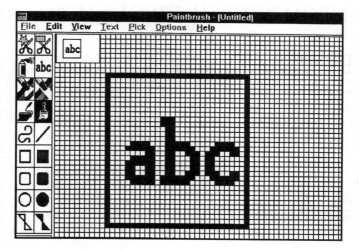

Bleed

Bleed is a printing term. It refers to printing that goes right to the edge of a page.

If you are working on a document that has a bleed, it means that the type or illustration in your document appears at the physical edge of your page. To reproduce artwork with a bleed using offset printing (see PRINTING, page 108), you need to supply the printer with the correct camera-ready artwork (see MECHANICAL, page 97). Artwork that bleeds must extend ⅛" *past* the edge of the page. This is so your bleed will print correctly, even if your artwork shifts slightly while being printed or trimmed. (It happens).

DEMONSTRATION

This is a business card with a bleed at the top and bottom:

COMPUTER TIPS

• If you are using output from a desktop printer and you plan to take it to a print shop, you may not be able to create a bleed. Most desktop printers will not let you print right up to the edge of a document. Keep this in mind when you plan your document.

Blend

A blend is made of graduated shades that progress smoothly from dark to light.

A blend is a design effect that can be used many ways: as a fill in a box, as a type effect, or as a background to add an overall tone to a page. When used properly, it gives a sophisticated and contemporary touch to your artwork.

Blends are created by gradually varying the density of shading within a given area. Because a blend is made of varying densities of dots, the issue of halftone screens enters into the printing of a blend (see HALFTONE, page 66).

To print a good blend, you will need a printing device that can handle grayscale printing. *You will have to experiment to get a good blend to print from a low-resolution printer.* The actual size of your blend, the starting and ending tones, the resolution of your printer, and the halftone screen your program uses, will all determine the quality of your blend.

DEMONSTRATION

This is an example of two types of blends:

This is a linear blend.

This is a radial or circular blend.

COMPUTER TIPS

- Different applications give you varying degrees of control over blends. If your program lets you specify beginning and ending tones for your blend there are a few things you need to know:

  The darkest end of your blend should not exceed 90%. A tint (or shade) of 90% will appear black, but the screen will not fill in or become muddy. The lightest end should be a fill of not less than 5%.

  If you plan to have your artwork printed by a print shop, keep in mind that blends tend to print to paper *darker* than they appear on your screen.

  If you have more tonal transitions than your printer can handle, you will get *banding*. That is when your blend breaks up into bands of gray (or whatever color you are using). This is an example of banding:

  The only way around banding is to either reduce your halftone screen setting, or decrease the tonal range of your blend (in other words, instead of blending from 20% to 90% shades, blend from 20% to 70%). The higher resolution output device (see RESOLUTION, page 122), the better results you will have with blends.

- More advanced desktop publishers who are working in color can create an attractive effect by blending one color with another.

**See HALFTONE, page 66
to learn more about blends.**

Body Copy

Body copy is the main text of a story or article.

Body copy does not include headlines. It is the small copy, usually between 8 and 11 pt., that makes up the bulk of your story or article.

DEMONSTRATION

These are examples of what body copy looks like:

Our most popular tour offers sightseeing excursions to the Imperial Capitals of Morocco, as well as side trips to sites of historical or scenic interest such as Moulay Idriss, the Roman ruins of Volubilis, and the Atlas Mountains.

This is 9 pt. Palatino Regular.

One of downtown's biggest employers announced that they would move their world wide headquarters out of the area within two years. The news came as a surprise to the twelve hundred employees who reported for work as usual today.

This is 8 pt. Helvetica Medium.

DESIGN TIPS

- Body copy is meant to be *readable*. When you select a typeface to use as body copy, consider both the nature of your project and your potential readers. Don't use body copy that's too small for your readers to comfortably enjoy.

Bold

Bold is type with a heavier, darker appearance than regular text or medium weight type.

Bold type is usually used in headings and titles, or to call attention to a particular group of words or names.

Most type families provide a bold version of their basic typeface, along with a medium or regular weight. Some type families come with several different kinds of bold — you might find an ultra-bold, extra-bold, heavy, black, or demi-bold in some families.

DEMONSTRATION

Here are some various weights of common typefaces:

Helvetica Medium	Century Light
Helvetica Bold	Century Book
Helvetica Heavy	**Century Bold**
Helvetica Black	**Century Ultra**

DESIGN TIPS

- Use bold type for emphasis within a passage of text. If there is a particular thought or concept you wish to highlight, try bold type. **Bold type conveys importance.** Use it to highlight important points.

- Try not to use bold type for large blocks of text since it is difficult to read in large passages. Bold type set in all capital letters is even more difficult to read. Use this feature sparingly.

Continued

11

BOLD

- Besides headlines, you can use bold type within a block of copy to highlight a proper name or title that appears recurrently — the name of a newsletter for instance.

- You can also use bold to highlight proper names within a story. Here is an example of an effective use of bold type from the Henry Hawthorne College Alumni News:

Where Are They Now Department

Good news from **Vanessa Carter**, who was just promoted to Vice President of RLK Investment Partners. She and **Jacqueline Hanover** had lunch the other day and invite all alumni to give them a call if they're in the Tacoma area.

Jonathan Van Albers reports his trip to China was the trip of a lifetime, and we hope he'll be bringing photos to the next reunion. **Barbara Apple**, **Kim Sands**, **Kelly Holmes**, and **Janice Gold**, were all bridesmaids at the wedding of **Jackson Reynolds** and **Tina Campbell**. To the happily married couple, congratulations!

This is 10 pt. Century Book type with Century Ultra.

**See TYPESTYLE, page 177
to learn more about bold type.**

Border

A border is a decorative frame that runs around type or pictures.

A border can be practical or decorative. You can use them to identify and call attention to certain information, or to make a page more lively and interesting.

Different applications let you apply borders in different ways; most desktop publishing programs come with a built-in set of borders, but allow you to import graphics, including more elaborate or unusual borders.

DEMONSTRATION

Here are some examples of common border styles:

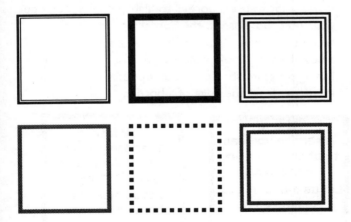

DESIGN TIPS

- You can give your borders variety by using different line weights and shading (see SHADE, page 147).

Continued

BORDER

- If you do a lot of work that requires borders — ads, coupons or certificates, for example — you can find some decorative and unusual borders in clip art collections. Here are some examples of clip art borders:

- If you want to use a border to highlight type, don't put your text too close to the border; give your text room to breathe. Type pushed up against the edge of a box does not look professional. Your desktop publishing program should have an option that lets you inset text from the edge of a border.

At last! **A service you can trust at a price you can afford.** **Let us make this tax season easy.**	*At last!* **A service you can trust at a price you can afford.** **Let us make this tax season easy.**
This is too tight.	This is better.

See CLIP ART, page 22 to learn more about borders.

Bullets

● ■ ✔

Bullets are typographic symbols used to call attention to selected lines or passages of copy.

You can use bullets to organize lists, add emphasis to a series of copy points, or as a device to separate blocks of copy.

Most fonts come with a bullet symbol (which is traditionally round). If you wish to use more unusual symbols as bullets, you can buy special symbol fonts that include bullets of all shapes and sizes.

DEMONSTRATION

Bullets vary in size:

- small bullet
● large bullet

Use bullets to organize lists:

Each tour includes:
- Round trip airfare
- Airport transfers
- Hotel accommodations
- Half-day sightseeing tour
- Departure tax

Use bullets to separate blocks of copy:

Terms and conditions for travel:

- Any change in the itinerary requested less than 30 days prior to departure shall be subject to a $25.00 per person penalty.

- All cancellations must be in writing.

- Trip cancellation insurance and health and accident insurance are strongly recommended.

Continued

DESIGN TIPS

- While bullets are usually round, there's no reason why any interesting symbol or dingbat (see DINGBAT, page 37) can't serve as a bullet. Some of the more commonly used bullets are:

  ■ Square bullets, for a modern, conservative look.

  ▲ Triangles, for a youthful, stylish look.

  ★ Stars, to add excitement.

  ✓ Checkmarks, for the look of a checklist.

- Depending on your project, you can use even more unusual bullets. If you have access to a symbol font — Carta, Wingdings®, Zaph Dingbats, Bill's Dingbats or one of many others — you can try using symbols like these as bullets:

   Thumbs up

  ❖ Tiles and patterns

  ♣ Printer's ornaments

  ♥ Hearts

  ✎ Pencils

  ☞ Pointers

  ⇨ Arrows

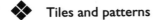

**See DINGBATS, page 37
to learn more about bullets.**

Call Outs

Call outs are selected short phrases from a story or article, enlarged and placed in the text as a highlight.

Also called *pull quotes*, a call out can be used to attract the reader's attention or interest, or to break up large blocks of text. A call out is also a name for the labels used to identify parts of an illustration.

DEMONSTRATION

Below is an example of a call out from a newsletter. It is used here to add intrigue to the story and hook potential readers. The quote used in the call out appears later in the article:

ONE MAN'S STORY

Many of you know Herman Gonzalez as the head of the King Housing Association. He's led the fight to raise standards of security in the King development and devoted many hours to improving the standard of living for tenants of the King development. But his efforts haven't been made without sacrifice.

"I heard you were tough," said the officer, as he helped Herman from the fire. "They were right."

Many of Herman's neighbors have heard the story of his brave efforts during last year's fire in the basement of 1200 Rogers Avenue. If you haven't heard it yet, it's another example of Herman's commitment to his friends and neighbors in mittment to his friends and neighbors in

(continued)

DESIGN TIPS

- There are many ways to make call outs interesting.
  Try reversing the type (see REVERSE page 128) or
  adding rules. You can also introduce different typefaces in your call outs:

**"If you plan to
Invest, make
sure you select
a mixture of
high-risk and
low-risk funds."**

*"IF YOU PLAN TO
INVEST, MAKE SURE
YOU SELECT A MIX-
TURE OF HIGH AND
LOW-RISK FUNDS."*

*i*f you plan to
invest, make sure
you select a mixture
of high-risk and
low-risk funds."

Capital Letters

Capital letters are used at the beginning of sentences. They also indicate proper names.

In desktop publishing, capital letters are often simply referred to as *caps*. Another term for capital letters is *uppercase* letters. If a block of copy is set in all capital letters, it is referred to as *all caps* or *all uppercase*.

DEMONSTRATION

These are capital letters:

ABCDEFGHIJKLMN

DESIGN TIPS

- Because capital letters are all the same size, unlike a mixture of capital and small letters, long blocks of copy set in all caps are difficult to read; try to avoid it. Notice how hard it is to tell capital letters apart at a glance:

  NORTH COUNTY GAS AND ELECTRIC WANTS
  TO HELP YOU CONSERVE ENERGY. THAT'S WHY
  WE'RE PROVIDING ALL OUR CUSTOMERS WITH
  A SPECIAL HANDBOOK, FULL OF TIPS ON HOW
  TO SPEND LESS ON ELECTRIC BILLS THIS YEAR.

- All capital, sans serif (see STYLE, page 142) letters (first heading) are easier to read than all capital, serif letters (second heading).

  MRS. BLOOM TO RETIRE THIS SPRING

  MRS. BLOOM TO RETIRE THIS SPRING

Charts and Graphs

Charts and graphs are ways of representing information symbolically.

The purpose of charts and graphs is to make it easy for the reader to absorb complex data. A glance at a pie chart, for example, can provide as much information as a full page of numbers. Charts and graphs are particularly effective at showing relationships between numbers because they allow you to make powerful visual comparisons. In the chart below, it is immediately obvious that more people traveled abroad in 1980 than in 1990.

Annual Number of Americans Traveling Abroad
(in millions)

DEMONSTRATION

There are many different kinds of charts and graphs.

Bar Chart   Stacked Chart   Pie Chart

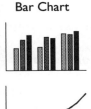

Line Chart   Area Chart   Scatter Chart

In addition to these, there are HLCO (High-Low-Close-Open), pictographs (charts which use pictures or symbols — see previous page), 3D graphics, and various combinations of all of the above charts.

DESIGN TIPS

- If you are creating a pie chart, your numbers or results should add up to 100% — not more.

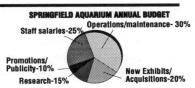

- Make sure you include a legend with your chart that explains your variables. Credit your information source.

- If you are trying to make a comparison between two numbers, make sure you create a graph that will demonstrate the differences. For example, in the first chart below, volume is measured on a scale of 1–50. This is too large; a scale of 1–7 is much more effective.

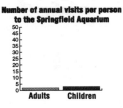 

Clip Art

Clip art is copyright-free graphics for use in your desktop publishing projects.

Clip art usually comes in collections organized by subject; the user just "clips" the illustration he or she wants. The collection may be electronic computer files on a disk or on CD-ROM, or printed clip art in a book. If you are using electronic clip art, you can import the picture into your word processing document or layout program. If you are using printed clip art and have a scanner, you can scan the artwork into the computer (see SCANNING, page 135). You can even paste clip art directly onto your *repro* (artwork you plan to repro-duce or print).

You can get clip art from any number of sources; you may already have clip art that came with your word pro-cessing program. If you have a scanner, the easiest place to start a clip art collection is an art supply store; many carry books of copyright-free art. They are usually orga-nized according to themes like sports, healthcare, humor, etc. Some are organized stylistically; you can find Art Deco, Japanese, Victorian, and Americana collections, to name a few. Below are some examples of clip art with a transportation theme:

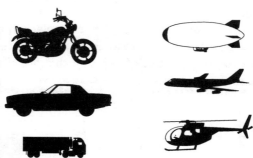

There are several clip art services you can subscribe to that will send you packages of electronic clip art each month. Or you can obtain copyright-free clip art from on line services such as CompuServe® or America Online®.

Clip art is one of the best resources a desktop publisher has. Use clip art to add life to a text-heavy page, to jazz up logos and headings, and to add visual impact to your message. But be aware that the issue of copyright is central when when it comes to illustrations of any kind; if you did not acquire the artwork in a legitimate exchange or purchase, don't use it! Scanning an illustration in a magazine is not clip art, and is *not* legal!

DEMONSTRATION

Below are some examples of clip art.

Clip art can be simple graphics:

Or more complex illustrations:

CLIP ART

You'll find clip art for many different themes, finance, travel, sports and animals among many others.

DESIGN TIPS

- It's never to soon to start a clip art library. Start to buy copyright-free art collections — either books or disks. It will make it easier to find just the right piece of art the next time you're in a rush and need an illustration.

- Use clip art creatively! Just because a piece of clip art is supplied to you in a certain way, doesn't mean you have to use it that way. Look for interesting ways to crop your artwork.

Clip art as provided.

How we used it.

COMPUTER TIPS

- If you deal with electronic clip art frequently, sooner or later you will need to understand file formats. Clip art comes in a variety of electronic forms and each form has its own rules regarding output, color, file size and other features. Before you buy a collection, you need to check what kind of format (see FILE FORMATS, page 47) your software supports, and what kind of format will produce the best results on your printer. Always make sure the clip art file is compatible with your program and printer.

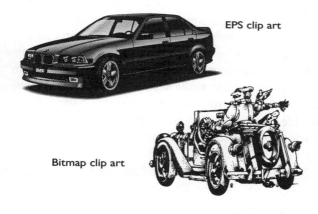

EPS clip art

Bitmap clip art

See GRAPHICS, page 56, FILE FORMATS, page 47, and SCANNING, page 135, to learn more about clip art.

Color Matching Systems

Color matching systems are standardized ways of describing colors by using numbered swatches.

Color matching systems exist so printers and commercial artists can communicate about color. By referring to a number and a swatch of color, a printer and graphic artist can be sure they are talking about the same color. If you pick a certain color for your stationery, for example, you want to make sure that the printer knows exactly what color you picked so that he or she can reproduce it exactly. Furthermore, if you reprint the job, you will want to know what color you used the first time.

Probably the most common color matching system is the PANTONE® system. PANTONE® makes many types of color guides to suit various materials and printing methods. Other popular systems used to identify color are TRUMATCH® and FOCALTONE®.

DEMONSTRATION

Here is an example of what a PANTONE® color swatch would look for a shade of gray:

DESIGN TIPS

- Be precise when specifying color. Color matching systems exist so you can get the *exact* color you want.

- Most printers will be able to show you a swatch book or a color specifier using one of the above-mentioned systems.

- More advanced layout and type programs include a dialog box that lets you specify colors in your document using the various color matching systems. Here is an example of a dialog box for color editing from QuarkXPress®. As you can see, the dialog box lets you select from among several color models:

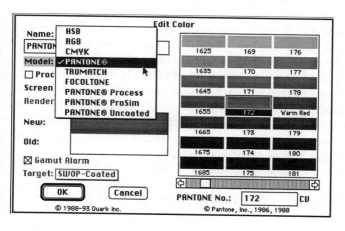

- Note that HSB, RGB and CMYK are other models for describing color. HSB stands for Hue, Saturation, and Brightness. RGB stands for Red, Green, and Blue. CMYK stand for Cyan, Magenta, Yellow, and Black, the four colors of process printing (see COLOR OFFSET PRINTING, page 28).

Color Offset Printing

There are two types of color offset printing: *process* **printing and** *flat* **or** *spot* **color printing**

In flat printing, pre-mixed color inks are used to print line art — solid areas of a single color — in this way, adding areas of color to a printed piece. The colors are usually specified as *Pantone colors* (see COLOR MATCHING SYSTEM, page 26). A typical flat color job might be printed in two colors — often black and a PMS (Pantone) color. The color would appear in certain limited spots, in the headings or in an initial cap for example. Tints or shades of a color can be created and printed in this process, but in flat color printing you are limited to a predefined set of colors, usually two or three. Newsletters, business cards, stationery, and inexpensive hand-outs or flyers are usually printed this way.

Process printing is also called four color printing or most generally, *color printing*. This is true full-color printing; it is how color photographs and full color illustrations in catalogs, books, and magazines are printed.

In this method, four basic inks called *cyan, magenta, yellow and black* mix in varying densities of dots. They combine to recreate the full range of colors. In order to print full color, you need to make a color separation of your artwork and break the image into its four component parts, the cyan, magenta, yellow and black plates. The four process colors never change, though the pictures you reproduce may vary.

Full color printing is a complex field, and if you are considering printing a project in full color, it is a good idea to discuss your job with a printer *before* beginning.

Columns

Columns are a way of dividing text on a page into vertical blocks. Columns break up a page into more readable segments. They are a

Columns are a way of dividing text into vertical blocks.

Columns break up a page into more readable segments. They are a good alternative to setting copy in one big block. A column of type is easier to read because there are fewer words on a line; readers tend to lose their place when lines of text are too wide.

Some programs call text that runs from the bottom of one column to the top of the next *newspaper columns* or *snaking columns*.

DEMONSTRATION

This is a page of text set in three columns:

Your Heading

Divide a page into columns Copy appears here in your columns, flowing from the base of one column to the

your call out can appear here, in one of your columns

top of the next column. Your grid is a basis for your design. You can divide a page into columns many ways, combining them for a double

Copy appears here in your columns, flowing from the base of one column to the top of the next column. Your grid is a basis for your design. You can divide a page into columns many ways, combining them for a double column width when you choose. Copy appears here in your columns, flowing from the base of one column to the top of the next column. Your grid is a basis for your design. You can

Copy appears here in your columns, flowing from the base of one column to the top of the next column. Your grid is a basis for your design. You can divide a page into columns many ways, combining them for a double column width when you choose. Copy appears here in your columns, flowing from the base of one column to the top of the next column. Your grid is a basis for your design. You can divide a page into columns

5

Continued

DESIGN TIPS

- If you are working in a format of three, four, or five columns, you can set some of your text to a two column width (or some other combination) in order to break up the uniformity of the layout and add variety.

- The smaller the size of your type, the narrower your column width should be. Columns should average somewhere between four to ten words per line for maximum readability.

- You can put a *rule* between columns for a nice design effect. The rules between columns should be thin — not larger than 1pt. (Some programs allow you to do this automatically.)

Condensed Type

Condensed type is type whose width has been compressed.

The characters of a condensed typeface are narrower than the regular typeface. Because the width of a letter is narrower, you can fit more characters per inch.

Condensed type is good when you have a lot of copy to fit in a small space.

DEMONSTRATION

This is Helvetica.

This is Helvetica Condensed.

Many layout programs let you condense or scale a typeface yourself. Scaling is measured in percentages: 100% equals the full, normal width of the letter.

100%, no scaling:	If you have too much copy, think about editing!
90% Horizontal scaling:	If you have too much copy, think about editing!
80% Horizontal scaling:	If you have too much copy, think about editing!
70% Horizontal scaling:	If you have too much copy, think about editing!
60% Horizontal scaling:	If you have too much copy, think about editing!
50% Horizontal scaling:	If you have too much copy, think about editing!

Continued

DESIGN TIPS

- A typeface that has been scaled by a word processing program or layout program is *not* the same as a typeface specifically designed (by a type designer) as a condensed typeface. A typeface specifically designed to be condensed is always superior in design and readability to a regular typeface that has been scaled.

- If you are working on a project that has a lot of text that needs to fit in a tight space, try using condensed type. If you don't have access to a condensed typeface, you can scale your type (if your program allows it), but try not to scale type too much — machine scaled type becomes difficult to read. Tracking and kerning are other tools you can use to help fit type into a tight space. (See TRACKING, page 168, or KERNING, page 80.)

ABOUT YOUR NEW HEALTH CARE PLAN

We want to work with you to curtail rising health care costs. That's why we are hard at work on a new flexible benefits program that allows each member to design his or her own unique health plan. Planning wisely now is the key to a healthy future.

10.5 pt. Palatino, condensed (scaled) 90%.

ABOUT YOUR NEW HEALTH CARE PLAN

We want to work with you to curtail rising health care costs. At the same time, we want to continue to offer affordable benefits to all our members. Therefore, we are hard at work on a new flexible benefits program that allows each member to design his or her own unique health plan. Planning wisely now is the key to a healthy future.

10.5 pt. Palatino, condensed (scaled) 60%.

The type condensed to 60% is almost illegible.

Copy

Copy refers to the raw material of desktop publishing — words.

You may have plenty of fancy typefaces, clip art and equipment, but before you can use any of it, you need copy. Copy is another word for text, but it is slightly more specific; copy is text as used in a commercial sense. If you are doing an ad, leaflet, invitation, newspaper or brochure, you are working with copy. If you are writing a journal, a report or a thesis, you are working with text.

A professional writer who supplies copy for ads and other commercial projects is called a *copywriter*.

Whether you get copy from a copywriter, your boss, your client, or your own imagination, when it first comes to you in an unformatted condition it is referred to as *raw copy*.

Raw copy is text for your desktop publishing project before it has been styled or typeset. It can be handwritten, typed, or placed on a disk.

DEMONSTRATION

When you start a desktop publishing job, you usually start with raw copy. It might look like one of these two samples:

This is ~~really~~ very sloppy raw copy. Give it back to whoever wrote it. It is not acceptable.

```
This is better.
Raw copy should be
supplied to you in
a readable form,
typed or neatly
handwritten.
```

Crop Marks

Crop marks are the marks in the corners of a mechanical (the art you prepared for a professional printer — see MECHANICAL, page 97) that show how a piece of artwork should be trimmed.

All artwork that is meant to be printed in a print shop and then cut to size should have crop marks. Crop marks must indicate both the horizontal and the vertical cut.

Crop marks should begin ⅛" of an inch from the outer edge of your artwork so that they do not accidentally show up in the artwork once your job is printed.

DEMONSTRATION

Here is a business card with crop marks (75% of actual size). Note that if you are preparing a piece of artwork for printing and you have put crop marks in position, you do not need a rule to outline your art:

Francine Millner
Senior Design Consultant

1234 MULBERRY STREET #10 • COUCHBERG, PA 56789
TEL. (232) 555-9000 • FAX (232) 555-9999

**See FOLD MARKS, page 50
to learn more about crop marks.**

Cropping

Cropping is the way you trim an image.

Cropping does not necessarily have anything to do with changing the size of a graphic; rather, it is determining which parts of an image should be included in your artwork, and which parts should not.

You might choose to crop an image because you need to make it fit in limited space. Or, you might crop an image in order to eliminate the unattractive or unnecessary parts of the picture.

DEMONSTRATION

This is an example of a picture that has been cropped:

DESIGN TIPS

• Crop in order to create a more powerful image.

Continued

CROPPING

- Crop in order to change the orientation of a picture. Here we took a horizontal photo and changed it to a vertical format:

- Keep in mind that if you are working to fit an image in a fixed space, you can crop your picture in order to make a selected part of it larger. Here we cropped the picture in order to make the woman's face larger.

Dingbat

A dingbat is a typographic ornament.

Dingbats are small graphics. Also called *printer's ornaments*, they can be used either decoratively or functionally. Some of the ways you can use dingbats are:

- To indicate the end of a story.
- To decorate titles.
- To separate sections in an article or story.
- To accent pages containing minimal text.
- As bullets.

In desktop publishing, dingbats are treated as text characters, not as graphics. This makes them very easy to use; you can access them right from the keyboard and treat them as you would any other text character.

There are dingbat fonts available from various manufacturers. Most word processing applications come with their own font or *character set* of dingbats.

DEMONSTRATION

These are examples of dingbats:

Use them to accent text:

CHAPTER 1

A Visit to Italy

Continued

DESIGN TIPS

- Dingbats provide a subtle decorative effect and are generally used in small sizes. Experiment by using dingbats in a larger size for some creative effects. You can also incorporate a dingbat into a logo design if you need a quick graphic.

- You can use dingbats to create a border by repeating them in a line.

❤❤❤❤❤❤❤❤❤❤❤❤❤❤❤❤❤❤❤❤❤❤❤❤❤❤❤❤

Mr. Wather's
WEATHER REPORT
☂ ☂ ☂ ☂ ☂ ☂ ☂ ☂ ☂

Display Cap

This is the large decorative capital letter at the beginning of a story or paragraph.

The purpose of display caps (or *display initials* as they are also called) is ornamental. Like many design elements, its main purpose is to break up the "grayness" of large blocks of text and attract the reader's eye to the beginning of the story.

There are different types of display caps. The more common styles are *drop cap, raised cap* and *hanging cap*.

DEMONSTRATION

A drop cap looks like this:

 eady to take that first step on the road to higher education? High school seniors are invited to Henry Hawthorne College this Saturday to participate in **Career Day**.

A raised cap looks like this:

eady to take that first step on the road to higher education? High school seniors are invited to Henry Hawthorne College this Saturday to participate in **Career Day**.

A hanging cap looks like this:

eady to take that first step on the road to higher education? High school seniors are invited to Henry Hawthorne College this Saturday to participate in **Career Day**.

Continued

DESIGN TIPS

- A display cap can be a modest type effect, or it can be a central aspect of your design; you decide. To add life to an initial cap, try experimenting with different typefaces for your initial cap. Or try a different use of type — an italic initial cap instead of a roman (upright) letter. You can introduce different shades or even a different color into your initial cap.

Ready to take that first step on the road to higher education? High school seniors are invited to Henry Hawthorne College this Saturday to participate in **Career Day.**

*M*other's day means flowers at Marguerita's gifts. How about a beautiful silk flower arrangement, customized just for her?

*W*e want to work with you to curtail rising health care costs. At the same time, we want to continue to offer affordable benefits to all our members.

Display Type

ABC

Display type is decorative type that is used primarily for headings and other large-size copy.

Display type is ornamental and eye-catching, as opposed to highly readable. It is used mainly for headings, signs, posters, logos, and short phrases.

Historically, display type is above 14 pt. in size. Because of its limited use — it was almost never used as body copy — display fonts were manufactured in only a few sizes without many special characters (see SPECIAL CHARACTERS, page 160).

Today, due to the nature of digital type, most fonts can be used in any size. But display fonts are still often designed only with uppercase letters and basic punctuation. They are usually designed only in one weight (i.e., they do not come in bold *and* regular).

Word processing, layout, and desktop publishing programs generally do not differentiate between display fonts (the actual computer file of your typeface) and standard text fonts because there is no physical difference between the two, as there was in the days when fonts were made of wood and metal. But it is still a useful distinction for a graphic designer.

A good type collection should have a healthy variety of both standard text fonts and more elaborate display fonts. Use the fancier typefaces when you need to add a little spice to your document, or when you are designing something (such as a logo) that needs a distinctive look.

Continued

DEMONSTRATION

Here are some examples of display fonts:

BODEGA

COTTONWOOD

FLINTSTONE

KANBAN

PRITCHARD

RITZ

RUBBER STAMP

SCRIBA

SUPERSTAR

VARGA

The above fonts come from a variety of manufacturers and sources, including Adobe Systems, Inc., Letraset, Bitstream, Inc., and public domain. As you can see, the name of the typeface often reflects the look or feel of the typeface.

DESIGN TIPS

• Avoid a classic mistake: Don't use display faces as body copy. They are not designed to be readable at small sizes. Here's what can happen:

> Photo plaza is offering a special two-for-one sale to celebrate the beginning of summer. Bring in one roll of film and get two sets of prints. You only pay for one.

• While it is tempting to use display fonts, try to select an appropriate typeface for your project. If you don't, your choice of typeface may look odd:

RLK INVESTMENT PARTNERS
SUE'S NEEDLEPOINT SHOP

Because display fonts usually convey a particular mood or feeling, stay with the ones that you think will be appropriate for your business or company.

**See TYPEFACE, page 171,
to learn more about display type.**

Dot Leaders

A dot leader is a row of dots that visually connects pieces of information.

Dot leaders help readers follow information across a page. Use dot leaders for prices in a catalog, contents, price lists and other tabular (tabbed) information (see TABS, page 164).

DEMONSTRATION

A leader can also be made of dashes or a solid line. Here are some typical uses of leaders:

SPRING SALE:
Begonia ....$ 6.99 each
Peony ....$19.99 each
Geranium.................$ 5.99 each

Set of matching oversized mugs
Available in Teal, Gray, Salmon, and White
Item #4201 ....$8.99 per set

Chapter 1.................................... Introduction
Chapter 2............. Cell Biology; A Small World

Name _____ Date _____

COMPUTER TIPS

- Some programs create a leader by filling the length of a tab with a character. You can change the size of the dots themselves by increasing the size type used for the fill.

Drop Shadow

A drop shadow is an effect which gives the illusion that a letter or word is three dimensional.

Most desktop publishing and word processing programs have a menu selection that automatically creates a drop shadow. This style is usually called *shade* or *shadow* on the menu selection.

DEMONSTRATION

This type has a drop shadow.

Note that the shadow is a tint or reduced percentage of the front color (in this case black).

Some drawing programs let you control the tint of the shadow and the degree of offset.

DESIGN TIPS

- Make sure the type is not kerned or tracked too tightly, otherwise the shadows might overlap and look blotchy.

Too tight!

DROP SHADOW

- Drop shadows add dimension and depth to a page. They make very effective headings on posters, signs and ads:

Let's Dance

The Edison Grand Hotel
*   invites you to an evening*
*   of ballroom dancing!*

SALE!

1/2 off on all snow tires

THE CALISTOGA THEATER CO. PRESENTS

South Pacific

A Musical Production

See DISPLAY TYPE, page 41,
to learn more about drop shadow.

File Formats

A file format is the way your program writes the instructions representing your file.

File formats are data structures; they are the organizing method your program uses to assemble the information you have created. The file format of your document allows one program to recognize a file that was created in another program.

There are many different file formats. The most basic format is ASCII (American Standard Code for Information Interchange), which is universal code for representing data. ASCII is straight alphabetical text that can be read by almost any program. ASCII is a *standard file format* because it can be read by many different programs. *Native* or *proprietary file formats* are unique to the program that created them. They are not generally read by other programs without the help of a translator.

There are many file formats which reproduce both graphics and text. Certain file formats are readable by most computers — PCs, MACs, Amigas and other systems. Many file formats are unique to a particular platform or system.

DEMONSTRATION

Below are types of different text and graphics file formats.

ASCII
AutoCAD
BMP

Continued

47

FILE FORMATS

EPS
HP Graphic Language
Giff
IFF
JIFF
JPEG
Lotus 1-2-3 Graphic
PC Paintbrush
PICT
RTF (Rich Text Format)
TIFF (Tagged Image File Format)
Windows Metafiles

The most important purpose of file formats is that they allow your document to be translated and used within various programs. This is particularly important for graphics files because they are frequently imported into other programs.

COMPUTER TIPS

- Not all programs read all file formats. If you plan to import data or graphics in a desktop publishing project, make sure you know what file formats are recognized or preferred by your program.

**See GRAPHIC, page 56, BITMAP, page 6
to learn more about file formats.**

Flush Left Flush Right

When a block of copy is lined up along its left margin, it is said to be *flush left*. When it is lined up by its right margin, it is called *flush right*.

These are traditional typesetting and graphic design terms. In desktop publishing, flush left and flush right are also referred to as *left aligned* and *right aligned*.

DEMONSTRATION

This is an example of copy that is flush left:

ABOUT YOUR NEW HEALTH PLAN

We want to work with you to curtail rising
health care costs. That's why we are hard
at work on a new flexible benefits program for
you and your family.

This is an example of copy that is flush right:

ABOUT YOUR NEW HEALTH PLAN

We want to work with you to curtail rising
health care costs. That's why we are hard
at work on a new flexible benefits program for
you and your family.

**See ALIGNMENT, page 2
to learn more about flush left and flush right.**

Fold Marks

Fold marks are marks on a mechanical or repro (the artwork you are preparing for a print shop — see MECHANICAL page 97) that indicate to a printer how to fold your document.

They are traditionally represented as broken or dashed lines that appear ⅛" of from the edge of your mechanical.

DEMONSTRATION

This is an example of a mechanical with fold marks. These marks indicate that this two page spread should be folded in half down the middle.

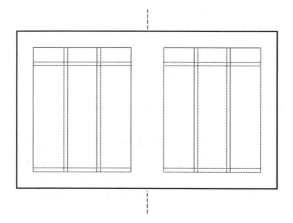

**See MECHANICAL page 97
to learn more about fold marks.**

Font

A font is a full set of symbols, letters, numbers and punctuation marks of one typeface.

Traditionally, the word *font* referred to a full set of characters in *one size only*. That was because printers needed a complete set of letters, or font, for each size type they wished to use. In the early stages of desktop publishing, a font referred to the same thing: a set of characters of one size and one style.

Today, with innovations in computer type, the word *font* is often used interchangeably with the word *typeface*. The difference is that the word *font* retains the more physical sense of being a complete set of characters, numbers and symbols (in digital form) while the word *typeface is* more intangible, referring to the unique appearance of a particular set of characters.

You purchase fonts from a font manufacturer. Most fonts come with a full set of upper- and lowercase letters, numbers zero through nine, basic punctuation marks, special symbols, fractions and accent marks.

DEMONSTRATION

This is an example of a font that includes a full set of characters, numbers and punctuation:

Palatino Regular
abcdefghijklmnopqrstuvwzxyz
ABCDEFGHIJKLMNOPQRSTUVWZXYZ
1234567890
(.,:;?!/ &%$¢*"''''{})

Continued

COMPUTER TIPS

- There are different font technologies available in the world of desktop publishing. The most common three are bitmap fonts, PostScript® fonts, and TrueType® fonts.

Bitmap fonts draw type by defining the letterform on a grid of pixels. Each letter in a bitmap font is mapped to a grid which corresponds more or less to the resolution of your monitor. Bitmap fonts are often jagged (they have rough, stepped edges). This is because they require a separate printer font for each type size. If you use a typesize for which you don't have a printer font, you get jagged letters. These ragged edges are called *jaggies*.

PostScript fonts are called scalable or outline fonts. They are drawn mathematically and so can be reproduced at any size; they require only one printer font to represent all sizes. They produce sharp, high quality letters, and are the standard among professional designers. PostScript fonts come with two parts: a screen font, which is a bitmap font, and a printer font.

TrueType fonts are another kind of scalable font that reproduce well at many different sizes and resolutions. They too use a bitmap as a screen representation, but are capable of printing well at any size. TrueType fonts produce particularly good results on non-PostScript printers.

oops! oops!

This is smooth type.   This is jagged type.

**See TYPEFACE, page 171,
to learn more about fonts.**

Footer

A footer is information that appears at the bottom of your page, below the main text in the bottom margin.

A footer can include anything that you would like to repeat as reference on every page. Some of the material that can go into footers are:

- **Chapter name and number**
- **Title of document**
- **Section**
- **Date/time stamp**
- **Page number**
- **Project title**
- **Organization name**
- **Author's name**
- **Name of class/teacher/course**
- **Graphics, rule or logo**

A footer is meant to provide a quick and easy reference to let the reader know where he or she is, as well as provide information about the document.

DEMONSTRATION

These are examples of footers:

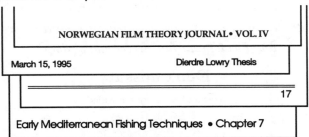

Formatting

When you format text, you apply a set of commands that define its appearance and position.

Until you start formatting type, you are merely typing. Once you start applying styles, selecting typefaces, setting tabs, choosing alignment, etc., you are formatting text.

DEMONSTRATION

This is unformatted text:

```
Wednesday Night is Caribbean Night at Cafe Bernice
Join us for a special tropical treat,
with live music and a delicious fixed-price buffet
dinner that includes our famous coconut shrimp!
Don't miss it.
Taxes and Beverages included.
```

This is formatted text:

Wednesday Night Is
Caribbean Night
at Café Bernice

Join us for a special tropical treat,
with live music and a delicious fixed-price buffet dinner
that includes our famous coconut shrimp!

Don't miss it.

Taxes and Beverages included.

DESIGN TIPS

- If you are formatting a large document that has recurring styles of text — for example, a style of heading that appears more than once — consider using *style sheets* (see STYLE SHEET, page 162).

- If you are using a lot of different kinds of formatting within your document, and you don't want to use style sheets, you may find it useful to write down your formatting information. Make a list of your various formats (also called *specs*) and keep it nearby. This way, if you should come across something that repeats, such as a heading, you won't have to search through your document to find an earlier example of the format. This will help you keep all your formatting consistent — a necessity in professional desktop publishing.

Your formatting instructions might look like this:

Styles for Newsletter

HEADS: 24 pt. bold Times Roman, centered, upper- & lowercase.

SUBHEADINGS: 14 pt. Helvetica regular, flush left, all caps.

BODY COPY: 9 pt. Times regular, justify. 12 pt. leading.

CAPTIONS: 8 pt. Times bold italic. Center under picture.

**See TYPESTYLE, page 177
to learn more about formatting.**

Graphic

A graphic, in desktop publishing, is a picture.

A graphic is anything that is not straight text. Illustrations, charts, symbols, halftones, maps, and cartoons are all examples of graphics.

Graphics are usually created in drawing or paint programs, or in applications that are specifically designed to generate charts and graphs. Graphics can also be scanned from hard copy, or purchased as clip art. In all of these cases, the graphic can then be *imported* or *placed* within a word processing or layout program, to be used in combination with type.

The purpose of graphics is twofold. First, a graphic is mean to visually support, dramatize, or elaborate what is communicated in the text. In this sense, it is an illustration. It should convey an aspect of the text that is perhaps better communicated visually than verbally. The illustration below, for example, uses financial symbols; it would be appropriate in an article on investment risks.

Second, a graphic is meant to break up text to give visual relief to the reader and provide a rest and diversion from long blocks of text. Make sure your graphic is doing at least one of these two things.

GRAPHICS AND FILE FORMATS

In desktop publishing, the electronic information that represents your picture (or text) is organized into a particular format or data structure. This is so that another program — one other than the one that created the graphic — might read and use the information. These various ways of representing graphic information are called file formats. They are the instructions that tell another application or device how to draw the graphic. If you want to understand desktop publishing fully, you need to understand the concept of file formats and learn which file formats are recognized by your application (see FILE FORMATS, page 47). Note that not all programs (or computer systems) are capable of reading all file formats.

Here is a list of some of the graphic file formats your program may recognize. Note that some are recognized by both PCs and Macs:

PC GRAPHICS FORMATS:

AutoCAD Format 2-D
AutoCAD Plot File
BMP
Computer Graphics Metafile
DrawPerfect
EPS (Encapsulated Postscript)
GIF (graphics Interchange Format)
HP Graphic Language
JPEG
Lotus 1-2-3 Graphic
Micrographix Designer/Draw
PC Paintbrush
(TIFF) Tagged Image File Format
Video Show Import
Windows Bitmaps
Windows Metafile
Zenographics Mirage

Continued

MAC GRAPHICS FORMATS:

Bitmap
EPS (Encapsulated Postscript)
GIF (graphics Interchange Format)
MacPaint
PICT
QuickTime movies
Photoshop
Pixar
TIFF
JPEG

OTHERS:

Scitex
IFF (Amiga)
TARGA
AGA (Amiga Graphics)
HAM
PhotoCD

DEMONSTRATION

Below are examples of different kinds of graphics.

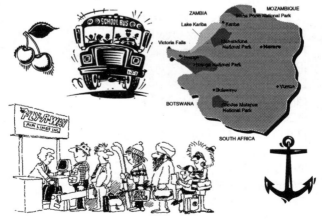

There are two general categories of graphics, from the point of view of printing:

LINE ART   This is artwork that is made of only one solid color (usually black). Logos are usually line art.

GRAYSCALE This is artwork that contains shades or tints. Another word for this kind of artwork is *continuous tone* or *halftone*. A photograph is an example of grayscale art.

DESIGN TIPS

• Be imaginative with your graphics. There are many
  ways to position graphics in relation to text.

Lorem ipsum dolor sit amet , consectetur adipiscing elit, sed diam nonumy eiusmod tempor incidunt ut labore et dolore magna

Lorem ipsum dolor sit amet , consectetur adipiscing elit, sed diam nonumy eiusmod tempor incidunt ut labore et dolore magna aliquam erat volupat. Ut einim as

Lorem ipsum dolor sit amet , consectetur adipiscing elit, sed diam nonumy eiusmod tempor incidunt ut labore et dolore magna aliquam erat volupat. Ut einim as minim veniam, quis

**See CLIP ART, pg. 22
to learn more about graphics.**

Graphic Design

Graphic design is the arrangement of graphics and text on a page so the page is both easy to read and pleasing to look at.

In even simpler terms, graphic design is visual communication. The graphic designer puts together a visual message for the reader, using the elements of words and pictures. The composition of words and pictures is then reproduced by some mechanical method such as offset printing or photocopying.

DEMONSTRATION

A graphic design project is rarely undertaken without some amount of planning. Even if the idea for a project arises spontaneously, there are certain aspects of the project that must be defined before any creative work begins.

On the next page is a checklist that includes some questions you must consider before beginning a design project. If you answer these questions at the beginning of the project rather than in the middle, you will save yourself the pain of costly mistakes, not to mention wasted time.

GRAPHIC DESIGN CHECK LIST

✓ **What is the message you wish to communicate?**

✓ **Who is your audience?**

✓ **How will your project be output? Will it be output to a laser printer? To slides? To overhead transparencies?**

✓ **How will your project be reproduced? Will it be printed? Photocopied?**

✓ **What is the budget for your work?**

✓ **Do you have a deadline?**

✓ **How many colors will you be using in this piece?**

✓ **How many pictures or illustrations?**

✓ **How much text?**

✓ **How will your project be distributed? Through the mail? Faxed? Modemed?**

These concerns or questions are common to all graphic design projects. You must consider them *before you begin,* in order to execute your job successfully.

DESIGN TIPS

• If you plan to do a job more than once — if you are doing a newsletter, for example — give your design project a consistent and distinct look. That way, each time your newsletter arrives, readers will recognize it.

Some of the elements that can repeat from project to project are: color, typeface, layout style, type effects like display caps, or a graphic element such as a logo.

See LAYOUT, page 83, THUMBNAIL, page 167, to learn more about graphic design.

Greek Copy

Greek copy is dummy copy that serves as a place-holder until more finished copy is available.

If you want to show your basic layout ideas to some-one — your boss or a client — before any copy has actually been written, try using greek copy. You can format greek copy just as you would regular copy.

Greek copy is usually in Latin or a made-up language so it is not a distraction to the reader. If you prefer, you can use some kind of repeating promotional copy.

DEMONSTRATION

This is an example of greek copy (also called *greeking*) as it might be used in a brochure layout:

Rilroth, LaTrege & Klieg
Quarterly Report

A Record Year for RLK

Lorem ipsum dolor sit amet, consectetur adipiscing elit, sed diam nonumy eiusmod tempor incidunt ut labore et dolore magna aliquam erat volupat. Ut einim as minim veniam, quis nostrud exercitation ullamcorpor suscipit laboris nisi ut aliquip ex ea commodo consequet. Duis autem est vel eum irure dolor in reprehenderit in voluputate velit esse molestaie consequat, vel illum dolore eu fugiat pariatur.

Grid

A grid is an underlying form upon which you base your design.

A grid breaks your page into symmetrical parts. When you create a grid, you lay all your text and graphic elements on top of this grid. In this way, you can be assured that all elements will line up and conform to an underlying structure; your page will look organized.

You can't actually see a grid in a final design. It is an organizational concept, a system you define to accommodate all your design elements. Create a grid by dividing up a page into even parts, either with paper and pencil, or with guidelines in a desktop publishing program. Then, follow this grid as you layout your text and graphic elements such as photos, charts, and illustrations.

In layout programs, you can create a grid in your *master pages*. Master pages are the user-defined default pages; they let you automatically position guidelines, columns, and other grid elements on every page.

DEMONSTRATION

Below are examples of grids.

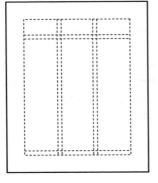
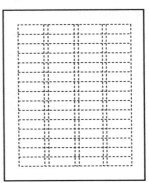

Continued

A grid usually divides a page symmetrically, with space for columns, headings, headers, footers, page numbers, and any other items that appears consistently.

DESIGN TIPS

- A grid is useful when you are doing a multi-page document, especially the kind that will be produced periodically, with different copy every time — a newsletter or a journal, for example.

- If you created a grid with pencil and paper, you can use tracing paper on top of it to sketch out how your various text and graphic elements will fit on the page. You can also buy pre-printed grids. These are printed in non-repro blue, a color that cameras and photocopy machines don't reproduce.

- You can "break" your grid by letting a graphic element go over the lines of the grid. This is a technique designers use to add life to a highly structured layout. You can even let your graphic go to the edge of your page, as in the example below.

Your Heading

Divide a page into columns. Copy appears here in your columns, flowing from the base of one column to the

your call out can appear here, in one of your columns

top of the next column. Your grid is a basis for your design. You can divide a page into columns many ways, combining them for a double.

Copy appears here in your columns, flowing from the base of one column to the top of the next column. Your grid is a basis for your design. You can divide a page into columns many ways, combining them for a double column width when you choose. Copy appears here in your columns, flowing from the base of one column to the top of the next column. Your grid is a basis for your design. You can

Copy appears here in your columns, flowing from the base of one column to the top of the next column. Your grid is a basis for your design. You

can divide a page into columns many ways, combining them for a double column width when you choose. Copy appears

5

**See LAYOUT, page 83,
to learn more about grids.**

Halftone

A halftone is a way of reproducing grayscale (continuous-tone) art by converting the various shades of gray into patterns of black dots. Taken together, these dots create the illusion of gray.

In graphic reproduction, a halftone is necessary in order to reproduce a picture or photograph. This is because most devices that print art in one color (including xerox machines, laser printers and imagesetters) do not actually print varying shades of gray — only black.

Halftone screens come in varying densities; the higher the lpi (lines per inch) of a halftone screen, the more detail is visible in the final screened image (see RESOLUTION, page 122).

Traditionally, a halftone was created by taking an image and photographing it through a screen printed with a pattern of dots. In desktop publishing, this process is done electronically. Advanced desktop publishing programs usually let you select the halftone screen resolution you wish.

A DEMONSTRATION

This is a halftone:

This is an example of various halftone settings:

45 lpi.   65 lpi   80 lpi

DESIGN TIPS

- If you are including a scanned photo in your project, it is important that you output it at the appropriate halftone screen setting (again, called *screen frequency* or lpi). Different methods of reproduction and printing require different halftone screen frequencies. Newspapers, for instance, are usually printed at 65 lpi or 85 lpi. Magazines accept screens as high as 133 lpi or 150 lpi. A 300 dpi laserwriter produces best results at a line screen of 60 lpi. Any line screen that is higher won't give as accurate a representation of your picture. (A new generation of screening technology, called *FM* or *stocastic* screening, will soon make it possible to get better detail with lower resolution devices).

**See SCANNING, page 135 and
RESOLUTION, page 122
to learn more about halftones.**

Hard Copy

Hard copy refers to a physical document — the kind you can hold in your hand.

If someone hands you a page of text for an ad, that's hard copy. If you print out a thirty page document in order to proof it or show it to someone, that's hard copy too. Hard copy is more comprehensive than the computer term *printout,* because it includes any physical page of text, not just pages printed from a computer.

DESIGN TIPS

• Always keep your original hard copy. You may need to refer to it later. It is also a good idea to proof your job in hard copy form because it is difficult to see certain types of errors on the screen.

**See PROOFING, page 119,
to learn more about hard copy.**

Header

A header is information that appears in the top margin of each page, above the text.

A header can include anything you wish. What makes it a header is that it appears on *each* page of your document. Some of the information that can be included in your header:

- **Chapter name and number**
- **Title of document**
- **Section**
- **Date/time stamp**
- **Page number**
- **Project title**
- **Organization name**
- **Author's name**
- **Name of class/teacher/course**
- **Graphics, rule or logo**

A header provides a quick and easy reference to orient the reader.

DEMONSTRATION

These are examples of a headers:

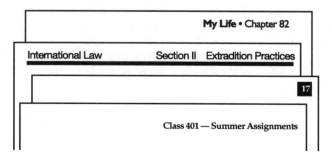

Headline

A headline is a large phrase that appears at the beginning of an article.

The purpose of the headline is to call attention to the story and entice the reader to read more. A headline should also provide some kind of summary of the contents for readers. Headlines usually have or imply a verb; otherwise they are just labels or titles.

DEMONSTRATION

Headlines should grab a reader's attention. Keep them short and direct. Make them meaningful.

RLK Partners to Leave City

CHICAGO. One of downtown's biggest employers announced today that they will move their world-wide headquarters out of the area within two years. The news came as a surprise to the twelve hundred employees who reported for work as usual today.

RLK announced the move at a press conference today in Chicago. Wanda Reynolds, spokesperson for the firm said the move did not reflect any dissatisfaction with the business climate in the area but that, "more attractive economic conditions elsewhere" were responsible for the company's decision.

DESIGN TIPS

- Select a typeface that is easy to read for headlines. It is usually the first thing readers will see. You don't want to lose readers early in the game by using a hard–to–read typeface.

- Once you pick a headline typeface, try to use the same typeface for all headlines throughout your document. You can make an exception of special sections, however, "Letters to the Editor," for instance, need not be considered a headline.

- You can set your headlines in several different sizes, with large headlines reserved for the most important articles. And remember, there is no law that says headlines need to be all capital letters. Caps and lowercase are easier to read than all caps.

    If you are using different sizes for your headlines, make sure you pick ones that are clearly different from each other. For example:

Major Headlines

This is 36 pt. Helvetica Condensed Black.

Secondary Headlines

This is 24 pt. Helvetica Condensed Black.

Minor or Third Level Headlines

This is 18 pt. Helvetica Condensed Black.

Hyphenation

Hyphenation is the breaking or splitting of words at the end of a line of text.

The importance of hyphenation is that it preserves and improves the readability of a block of justified text. Hyphenation permits your program to make adjustments to wordspacing and letterspacing on a line-by-line basis by breaking words to create more (or less) room on a line. Hyphenation gives your program flexibility to fit type.

Advanced layout programs allow users to define hyphenation settings. These are usually included under an option called, *H&J* (Hyphenation & Justification).

Hyphenation also helps control the appearance of type that is set flush left by making adjustments to the way type *rags* on the right. (See ALIGNMENT, page 2.)

Your program determines word breaks using algorithms and hyphenation dictionaries. These electronic decision-makers are not always right, however. When you find a peculiar, incorrect word break, or one that makes the word hard to read, it is called a *bad break*. Bad breaks interfere with reading and should be corrected manually. *Crac-ked, sop-histicated, new-spaper, psycologist* are examples of bad word breaks.

Hyphenated text should always be carefully proofread.

DEMONSTRATION

This is an example of hyphenated, justified text:

> A new school season will begin soon and we at the Fitzgerald Planetarium are looking forward to another year of learning. For us, a new school year means more exhibits, sky shows, and after-school programs to help students in their exploration of the universe.

DESIGN TIPS

- Don't hyphenate too many words in a row. It disturbs the appearance of your page and interrupts the reader's concentration. Two consecutive hyphenations should be the limit. Also, you should adjust the parameters or settings of your application so that only words of five or more letters are hyphenated.

- Do not a hyphenate a short phrase such as a headline, title, or short quote:

Truth is great and will prevail if left to herself.

Thomas Jefferson

In the above example, the force of the quote is disrupted by the word break. Compare it to this:

Truth is great and will prevail if left to herself.

Thomas Jefferson

Continued

HYPHENATION

- Use a soft or hard carriage return to send the hyphenated word to the next line. A hard carriage returns creates a new paragraph. A soft carriage return only breaks a line,

- If your text is full of hyphenated words, it means your line length (the width of a line of text) may be too short. Try increasing it in order to reduce the number of word breaks. For example:

The Café Morocco

In this dark thriller, Hughie Broderick plays Detective *Sammy Gum*, sent to explore a strange disappearance. When the detective explores the Café's back rooms, he learns the terrible secret of the Café's owner, Hans.

Not only does the above copy have too many hyphenations, it has too many broken proper names. Notice how much easier it is to read this copy:

The Café Morocco

In this dark thriller, Hughie Broderick plays Detective *Sammy Gum*, sent to explore a strange disappearance. When the detective explores the Café's back rooms, he learns the terrible secret of the Café's owner, Hans.

See JUSTIFICATION, page 79, to learn more about hyphenation.

Indent

When copy is inset from the left or right margin, it is indented.

Copy is usually indented to indicate a new paragraph. It can also be indented to set off lines from surrounding text, as in the case of a long quotation.

You can indent text on the left or the right. Another common indent is a *hanging indent* where the first line runs the full line length, and all following copy in the paragraph is indented.

DEMONSTRATIONS

Below are examples of various ways copy can be indented:

First line indent:

Lorem ipsum dolor sit amet, consectetur adipiscing elit, sed diam nonumy eiusmod tempor

Duis autem est vel eum irure dolor in reprehenderit in voluputate velit esse molestaie consequat, vel illum dolore eu fugiat nulla pariatur.

Left indent:

Lorem ipsum dolor sit amet, consectetur adipiscing elit, sed diam nonumy eiusmod tempor

Duis autem est vel eum irure dolor in reprehenderit in voluputate velit esse molestaie consequat, vel illum dolore eu fugiat nulla pariatur.

Continued

INDENT

Right indent:

> Lorem ipsum dolor sit amet, consectetur adip-
> iscing elit, sed diam nonumy eiusmod tempor
>
> *Duis autem est vel eum irure dolor in rep-*
> *rehenderit in voluputate velit esse molestaie*
> *consequat, vel illum dolore eu fugiat nulla*
> *pariatur.*

Left and right indent:

> Lorem ipsum dolor sit amet, consectetur adip-
> iscing elit, sed diam nonumy eiusmod tempor
>
> > *Duis autem est vel eum irure dolor in rep-*
> > *rehenderit in voluputate velit esse*
> > *molestaie consequat, vel illum dolore eu*
> > *fugiat nulla pariatur.*

Hanging indent:

> Lorem ipsum dolor sit amet, consectetur adip-
> iscing elit, sed diam nonumy eiusmod tempor
>
> *Duis autem est vel eum irure dolor in repre-*
> > *henderit in voluputate velit esse*
> > *molestaie consequat, vel illum dolore*
> > *eu fugiat nulla pariatur.*

DESIGN TIPS

- A hanging indent is often used to organize bulleted or numbered text. For example:

  - In this case the bullet is part of the first line (which extends past the rest of the indented copy).

  - ***Hanging Indent*** Here is another example of this method of indenting text. Use it for a glossary.

Input

Input is the what you put into your computer.

A keyboard, mouse, digitizing tablet, scanner and microphone are examples of input devices. They all do the same thing; they take information and send it into your computer as data. Once inside the computer, *all input is exactly the same.* It is digital information that your CPU (computer) can process any way you choose. It can pass the information along to your program, monitor, hard disk, or wherever your software dictates.

DEMONSTRATION

Below are examples of input devices.

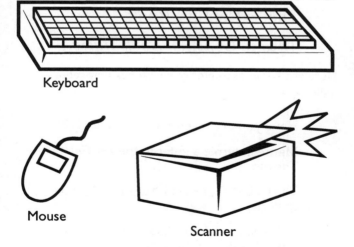

Keyboard

Mouse

Scanner

Italic

type

Italic refers to a typeface that slants to the right.

An italic typeface is usually related to a roman version (non-italic) of the same type family. Letterforms of an italic typeface are not merely roman letters tilted to the right (that is called *oblique*); they have their own unique design.

Italic type is generally used for emphasis within a passage of text. There are also certain types of information that should always be italicized: the names of publications (books, magazines and newspapers), the names of ships or trains, movie titles, and the titles of works of art. Foreign words and phrases should also be italicized.

DEMONSTRATION

This is Century Book.

This is Century Book Italic.

Here are some examples of sentences that require italic type:

Have you ever seen Monet's *Water Lilies?*

Maureen wrote a letter to the *The Chicago Tribune.*

The *Orient Express* still runs from Venice to Paris.

"*Mañana,*" said the clerk, when Juan asked when the next train would be leaving.

The Innocents Abroad is one of Mark Twain's wittiest books.

Justification

When a block of copy is justified, all lines of text begin at the same point on the left and end at the same point on the right.

In order to justify type, your program makes adjustments to each line of type. It adjusts the spaces between words, the spaces between letters, and the way words break at the end of the line. These adjustments are called *letterspacing, word spacing* and *hyphenation*. These typesetting basics determine the overall appearance of a block of type.

Sophisticated type and layout programs let users make adjustments to the program's settings for letterspacing, wordspacing and hyphenation, which in turn affect how the program justifies type.

Note that certain programs, including WordPerfect® use the term justification loosely, allowing it to refer to all forms of alignment. Traditionally, justification only refers to only one kind of alignment (shown below).

DEMONSTRATION

This is a block of type that has been justified:

> Ebenezer Bryce, the man who gave his name to Bryce Canyon, arrived in Utah in the 1870's. He described the canyon as "a heck of a place to lose a cow," an amusing description of an otherwise bizarre landscape. Strange, pink rock formations, formed when sediments were pushed upwards by the pressure of the earth, present visitors with eerie suggestions of stone giants.

**See ALIGNMENT, page 2
to learn more about justification.**

Kerning

Kerning is the adjustment of space between pairs of letters.

When you kern type, you move pairs of letters closer together or farther apart in order to create more pleasing and readable text. Kerning is done to give the impression of equal, balanced spacing between pairs of letters.

Kerning — also called *letterspacing* — is a vital part of typesetting and graphic design. There are thousands of possible combinations of the 26 letters of our alphabet, and sometimes awkward spaces occur between letters. Even though two letters might have exactly the same amount of space between them as between another pairs of letters, they may give the illusion of being varying distances apart. For example, the letters below seem to be farther apart in the first pair of letters than in the second pair:

OT   AT

Not all word processing programs give users the power to manually kern type, although many sophisticated type and layout programs do. Depending on the program you use, however, kerning might be measured in very tiny units of measures — $\frac{1}{200}$ of an em space for example (an *em space* is the width of the letter "M" in the font you are using) — or in bigger units such as fractions of a point.

Adjustments made to groups of letters or blocks of copy is called *tracking* or, in some programs, *letterspacing*. *NOTE: letterspacing is still an evolving concept in the world of desktop publishing; you will find slightly different definitions of kerning, tracking, and letterspacing from application to application.*

DEMONSTRATION

Here is a phrase set in 25 pt. bold capital letters:

TYPOGRAPHY

There appears to be extra space between the letter pairs, "O" and "P", and "P" and "H." After kerning:

TYPOGRAPHY

Here is a phrase set in 22 pt. bold capital letters:

ONE DAY ONLY SALE

It doesn't look bad, but notice how much more balanced the phrase appears, after kerning some of the letter pairs:

ONE DAY ONLY SALE

If you adjust the letterspacing of a whole line or block of text, and not just between pairs of letters, it is called *tracking* (see TRACKING, page 168)

DESIGN TIPS

• Some fonts have inherently poorer letterspacing than others and so require more adjustment — watch for this. If you are dissatisfied with the typeface you are using and don't want to put the time into kerning, consider picking another typeface.

- There is nothing that gives away poor design faster than bad kerning (or no kerning). It is most noticeable in headings. You have probably seen headings that look like this:

Sales Record Set This Year

Whenever possible, try to kern your headings.

Sales Record Set This Year

**See TRACKING page 168
to learn more about kerning.**

Layout

A layout is a preliminary study or sketch that shows how text and graphics will be arranged on a page.

A layout is a little bit like a blue print; your layout is the plan you follow as you assemble your artwork in the computer.

Here are some of the things you might want to include in your layout:

- **Headings**
- **Subheadings**
- **Body copy**
- **Graphics**
- **Captions**
- **Photos**
- **Logos**
- **Company information**
- **Coupons**
- **Borders**

There are several reasons why a layout is a valuable and essential step in all but the most simple graphic design projects. First of all, it is an opportunity to plan ahead. If you are doing a large document, you don't want to wait until you've formatted ten or twenty pages to find out that you should have used a three column format instead of two. A layout gives you the opportunity to work out certain design and space problems *before* you sit at the computer.

Secondly, a layout helps you understand your project. It is an opportunity for you, the designer, to consider what would be the best, most effective method of com-

Continued

design options as you create your layout.

There are two general kinds of layouts. A layout that is very precise with all elements clearly and neatly fit in and indicated down to the smallest detail is called a *tight layout*. A rough sketch that gives a general idea of how things fit is called a *loose layout*.

DEMONSTRATION

Below are some examples of layouts.

This is a loose layout:

This is a tight layout. The type, which is dummy or greek (see GREEK COPY, page 62), can be created on your computer. The illustrations are sketched in by hand. A tight layout is also called a *comp*.

DESIGN TIPS

- Layouts are an opportunity to explore and solve design problems. (Such as how to fit a lot of photos on a page, or what to do with too much copy.) People sometimes argue that doing a page at a computer is faster than sketching by hand. That's true for production work, but when it comes to problem solving, your brain is still faster. Use your layouts to explore different approaches to your project.

- A layout may be rough or sketchy in appearance, but it should be fairly precise in what it is describing. If you are sketching a layout by hand, make sure your layout (no matter how sloppy) reflects realistic choices. Sketch in pictures at an accurate size, measure margins and column widths. Be loose but precise. For example:

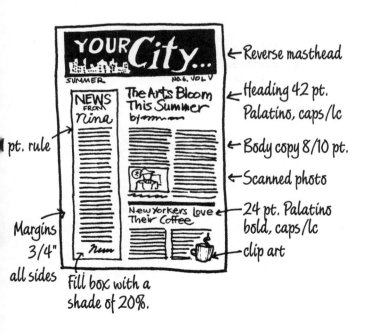

← Reverse masthead

← Heading 42 pt. Palatino, caps/lc

← Body copy 8/10 pt.

← Scanned photo

— 24 pt. Palatino bold, caps/lc

— clip art

1 pt. rule

Margins 3/4" all sides

Fill box with a shade of 20%.

Continued

LAYOUT

- *Be prepared to sketch something unsuccessful.* You can't get to a good working layout without making some bad choices or trying what *doesn't* work. Out of your dead-ends will come a terrific, workable solution.

- Look for a solution that is *flexible,* one that will accommodate the range of material you will be working with. For example, if you are going to be working with different headings, your layout should accommodate both long and short headings.

**See THUMBNAIL, page 167,
GRAPHIC DESIGN, page 60,
TYPEFACE, page 171,
to learn more about layout.**

Leading

Columns are a way of dividing text on a page. Columns break

Leading refers to the space between lines of copy.

Leading, pronounced "ledding," is determined by measuring the distance from the baseline of one line of text to the baseline of the next line of text (see BASE-LINE, page 5.). Another word for leading is *linespacing*.

Leading is a vital factor in readability. If lines of type are too close to each other or too far apart, it is hard for the reader to follow the flow of text.

Many word processing applications measure leading in *lines*. Most layout programs, however, use the traditional measurement of *points*. If you are working with 10 pt. type, the leading might be 12 pt. — indicating that there are two extra points of space between lines. Traditionally, this leading would be expressed like this:

$$10/12$$

The top number represents type size, the bottom number represents leading. This is an easy way of marking leading, should you want to make notes on your document, or include the information on a list of formatting styles.

In desktop publishing, there are several different ways to specify leading, again depending on the program. *Absolute* or *fixed leading* refers to the measurement from baseline to baseline, expressed in an *absolute* numerical form: for instance, 24 pt. leading is a fixed measurement. *Relative leading* refers to the distance between lines expressed as a positive or negative number, added to the type size, whatever it may be. For example, a setting of +2 will add two points to whatever type size you are currently using. Some programs express this relativity in percentages; a leading setting of 20% will add an additional 20% of your type size as leading. For example, 10 pt.

Continued

LEADING

type with leading set at 20% will add an additional two points to your type size. This same setting — 20% — would and additional eight points if applied to 40 pt. type.

Certain programs use a setting called *Auto*. This is another way of expressing relative leading. *Auto* means your program will automatically add 20% leading — or whatever default setting you select — to your type.

Explore the different ways your program specifies leading.

DEMONSTRATION

Here are some examples of different leading settings:

A good designer is willing to trust intuition, and is not afraid to use his or her own personal sense of taste. Good intuition is based on years of experience and much observation; each time you pick up something printed you can learn about design!

This is 9 pt. Helvetica type and 9 pt. (or +0pt) leading.

A good designer is willing to trust intuition, and is not afraid to use his or her own personal sense of taste. Good intuition is based on years of experience and much observation; each time you pick up something printed you can learn about design!

This is 9 pt. Helvetica type and 10 pt. (or +1pt) leading.

A good designer is willing to trust intuition, and is not afraid to use his or her own personal sense of taste. Good intuition is based on years of experience and much observation; each time you pick up something printed you can learn about design!

This is 9 pt. Helvetica type and 11 pt. (or +2pt) leading.

A good designer is willing to trust intuition, and is not afraid to use his or her own personal sense of taste. Good intuition is based on years of experience and much observation; each time you pick up something printed you can learn about design!

This is 9 pt. Helvetica type and 12 pt. (or +3pt) leading.

DESIGN TIPS

- For easy-to-read body copy, add two or three points of leading to the type size (depending on your typeface).

- Experiment with leading. There are no rules as to exactly how much leading you need; it depends on the typeface you have chosen, the length of your lines of text, the depth of your columns and the x-height of your typeface (see X-HEIGHT page 184.). The same leading setting with two different typefaces can have a very different visual effect. Let your eyes be the final judge of readability.

- Large size type such as headings, — especially all caps headings — require less leading. For example, a heading of thirty points might look better with *negative* leading:

ANNOUNCING OUR BIGGEST SALE EVER!

This is 20 pt. type and 22 pt. (or +2pt) leading.

ANNOUNCING OUR BIGGEST SALE EVER!

This is 20 pt. type and 18 pt. (or -2pt) leading.

- For an elegant look, try working with a very large amount of leading:

Marguerita's Gifts

invites you to review

our new line of

holiday treasures.

This is 9 pt. Century Book Italic with 14 pt. leading.

Logo

A logo, short for logotype, is a unique symbol created and used to represent an organization, person or product.

A logo serves an important purpose in graphic design. It is a company's visual calling card. It labels all products or services the organization provides, and appears on all correspondence, projecting the company's image.

A logo is made of some combination of type and/or graphics. Once designed, the logo should be used consistently on all products to assure recognition.

DEMONSTRATION

Below are examples of logos. As you can see, they can be composed of type alone, or include a symbol or graphic.

DESIGN TIPS

- A logo should reflect the mood or personality of the organization, person or company for which you are creating it.

- Be consistent. The color, shape, typeface, etc. of your logo should not change every time someone uses it. If you are working in a company with many people, make sure they are all aware of the standards for your logo. This is called *Logo Usage*.

- If you design a logo, make sure it works at different sizes. Below is a logo which looks fine at a fairly large size, but it's difficult to read when you reduce it to fit on a business card.

Madeline Productions
INTERNATIONAL
✳

Madeline Productions
INTERNATIONAL
✳

Lowercase ^{abc}

Lowercase is the typesetting term for small, uncapitalized letters.

The opposite of lowercase is *uppercase* — another term for capital letters.

DEMONSTRATION

These are lowercase letters:

abcdefghijklmnopqrstuvwxyz

DESIGN TIPS

- For a stylish look, try setting your copy in all lower-case letters. This works best with short advertising copy.

**this christmas,
smedley's wants to
take the guess-work
out of shopping.**

**See CAPITAL LETTERS, page 19
to learn more about lowercase.**

Margins

na aliquam erat volupat. Ut einim as minim veniam, quis nostrud exercitation ullamcorpor suscipit laboris nisi ut aliquip ex ea com-

Margins are the borders along the edge of your page where no type or copy appears.

There are margins on both the left and right of the page, and at the top and bottom of a page.

DEMONSTRATION

The margins are the areas around the copy.

Auto Show Coming to Convention Center

Lorem ipsum dolor sit amet , consectetur adip iscing elit, sed diam nonumy eiusmod tempor incidunt ut labore et dolore magna aliquam erat volupat. Ut einim as minim veniam, quis nostrud exercitation ullamcorpor suscipit laboris nisi ut aliquip ex ea commodo consequet. Duis autem est vel eum irure dolor in reprehenderit in voluputate velit esse molestaie consequat, vel illum dolore eu fugiat nulla pariatur.

At vero eos et accusam et iousto odogio dignissium qui blandit est praesent luptatum delenit aigue duos dolor et molestias excepteur sint occaecat cupidatat non provident, simil tempor sunt in culpa qui officia deserunt mollit anim id est er expedit distinct.

Nam liber tempor cum soluta nobis eligent optio est congue nihil impedit doming id quod

DESIGN TIPS

- A typical margin for an 8 $\frac{1}{2}$" x 11" page of text or publication is between $\frac{1}{2}$" (3 picas) and 1" (6 picas). For a lighter or airier look, try using a margin of 1 $\frac{1}{2}$."

- If you are creating a document with *facing pages* — a spread of two pages side-by-side — you should consider making the inside margins slightly smaller than

Continued

the outside margins. When the pages are next to each other, the white spaces of the inside margins (also called the *gutter*) run together and appear even larger.

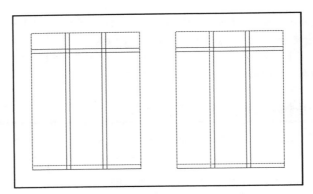

- When you create margins for your document, keep in mind the capabilities and limitations of your printing device. If you design a document with narrow margins, you may inadvertently place text in an area that your printer can't print (most desktop printers do not print right up to the edge of a page). Your text may be cut off when the document is printed. Watch where you position headers and footers.

Measurement

In graphic design and typesetting, the common units of measure are points and picas.

Points are the smallest unit of measure. There are 72 points in an inch. Type is measured in points, as is leading.

The larger unit of measure — the pica — is used for measuring the width of a line, the depth of a column or other large distances. There are six picas in an inch, and 12 points in a pica. Picas are often a preferable way of breaking up an inch into smaller units because they easily divisible.

Many desktop publishing programs allow great flexibility in choosing measurements. Some programs let you choose inches, picas, points, or even millimeters as units of measure. Programs with *rulers* (the measuring bars that run across the top and side of a window) often allow you to specify the units of measure on both the horizontal and the vertical axis.

Other units of measure you may encounter:

• **Agates** (or agate lines) are used to measure column depth in newspaper advertising.

• **Ciceros** are a European method of measuring the width and depth of a line of type.

• **Millimeters** and **centimeters** are standard measurements in the metric system, used outside the United States.

Continued

DEMONSTRATION

Below are comparative measurements of some of the common units of measure.

DESIGN TIPS

- Many word processing systems only use inches in their specifications and dialog boxes. There may be times when you wish to convert one unit of measure to another. Below is a chart that converts picas to inches:

POINT-INCH CONVERSION TABLE

The numbers on the left side of each column represents points. The numbers on the right side of each column are the inch equivalents.

PTS.	INCH	PTS.	INCH	PTS.	INCH	PTS.	INCH
1	0.014	22	0.306	43	0.597	64	0.889
2	0.028	23	0.319	44	0.611	65	.0903
3	0.042	24	0.333	45	0.625	66	0.917
4	0.056	25	0.347	46	0.639	67	0.931
5	0.069	26	0.361	47	0.653	68	0.944
6	0.083	27	0.375	48	0.667	69	0.958
7	0.097	28	0.389	49	0.681	70	0.972
8	0.111	29	0.403	50	0.694	71	0.986
9	0.125	30	0.417	51	0.708	72	1.000
10	0.139	31	0.431	52	0.722	73	1.014
11	0.153	32	0.444	53	0.736	74	1.028
12	0.167	33	0.458	54	0.750	75	1.042
13	0.181	34	0.472	55	0.764	76	1.056
14	0.194	35	0.486	56	0.778	77	1.069
15	0.208	36	0.500	57	0.792	78	1.083
16	0.222	37	0.514	58	0.806	79	1.097
17	0.236	38	0.528	59	0.819	80	1.111
18	0.250	39	0.542	60	0.833		
19	0.264	40	0.556	61	0.847		
20	0.278	41	0.569	62	0.861		
21	0.292	42	0.583	63	0.875		

Mechanical

A mechanical is the traditional term for artwork that has been prepared for the printing process.

Another word for mechanical is *camera-ready artwork*. At this stage, the artwork is ready to be shot by a camera and made into film — the next step in print production.

A mechanical has two basic functions:

- To provide all the actual artwork for the piece to be printed, including type, graphics and photos.

- To supply a set of instructions so the printer possesses all the relevant information about *how* the piece is to be printed.

In the first step — the preparation of artwork — the artist traditionally pastes pieces of type to a board. This hand-assembled art is called a *paste-up*, (still another word for mechanical). All type and art is black and white at this stage. The artist also positions pictures and illustrations or, more commonly, he or she positions *placeholders* for the pictures (such as a photocopy of the picture). Placeholders are used because the final picture is ultimately created by the printer. The placeholder is called *For Position Only* art, and is usually marked *F.P.O.*

In the second step, the artist writes instructions on tracing paper overlaying the board, or on the board itself. These instructions were and still are vital to successful printing because they contain information regarding any number of production features, such as:

- **Color break-up:** Indicates to the printer what art should be printed in which particular color.

Continued

MECHANICAL

- **Folding instructions:** Shows the printer where and how your artwork folds.

- **Cutting instructions:** Shows the printer how to trim your page to the correct size.

- **Tint indications:** Shows the printer what tints (shades) should be applied. A tint or shade of a color might be used to fill a box, or to create shaded type.

- **Instructions regarding photos:** Indicates sizing and cropping information, as well as information as to where the photo should be positioned.

- **Bleed indications:** (see BLEED, page 7)

Historically, a graphic designer was finished with his or her job when a mechanical was delivered to the printer. Today, the concept of mechanical is one of the most transformed aspects of graphic design. A hand-assembled board, covered with bits of type is no longer necessary. Computer-generated art allows the graphic artist to put all artwork and type in position *before* it is printed. Once the artwork is output (see OUTPUT, page 104), all that remains is to provide the printer with instructions as to how the job should be printed. Crop marks, fold marks and color indications are still required if you are supplying a printer with artwork.

More advanced desktop publishers may be familiar with the concept of film output. This allows you to circumvent mechanicals entirely. In this case, the printer can print the film he or she needs *directly* from the desktop publisher's computer file, following all instructions for color *within* the file itself.

For the time being, however, most desktop publishers will continue to create mechanicals from some kind of paper output.

DEMONSTRATION

A traditional mechanical might look like this. Indications and instructions for the printer would be written on an overlay on top.

DESIGN TIPS

- If you are working on a piece of artwork that you plan to print in a professional print shop, *ask the printer what kind of camera-ready artwork he or she needs from you.* Discuss photos and pictures, ask how your printer would like you to indicate color. Understand that printing is an entirely different process from desktop publishing. It has its own rules and its own requirements. You need to know what they are if you plan to prepare that project for printing. Always talk to your printer *before* you do your mechanical.

See PRINTING, page 108, OUTPUT, page 104, to learn more about mechanicals.

Moiré

A moiré is an unwanted pattern of dots that appears in a halftone (see HALFTONE, page 66).

A moiré is created when two different halftone dot patterns cross and create interference. This usually happens when you scan something that has already been printed as a halftone before. For example, if you try to scan a picture that has already been printed in a newspaper, there is a chance you may get a moiré pattern when you print it again. That's because it has been turned into a halftone — or *screened* — twice; once when it was printed in the newspaper and then again when you scanned it and printed it from your computer. The two sets of dots create a moiré pattern.

If you get a moiré pattern in a picture, you will know it, even if you don't understand how you got it. The only thing you can do about it is try one of the below suggestions:

1. Try to get a clean, unscreened original.

2. If you can't get a new original, scan your artwork at a different angle. Rotate it slightly on the scanning bed.

3. Try scanning your photo at a different size. If you can scan it at a smaller percentage, you may be able to minimize the pattern.

4. Scan your picture at a different resolution. Experiment until you have minimized the pattern. You can also experiment with your halftone screen frequency (lpi), if you are working in a program that allows it.

5. Use image retouching software to reduce the pattern. This is the most advanced solution, and probably the most effective (short of getting a new original).

DEMONSTRATION

This is an example of a picture with a moiré pattern:

Orphan

An orphan is a typesetting term. It refers to an awkward situation where the last line of a paragraph flows, alone, to the top of the next column.

It's called an orphan because it has been separated from the rest of the paragraph to which it belongs.

Graphic designers avoid orphans because they disturb the balance of a page and interrupt the flow of reading.

DEMONSTRATION

This is an example of an orphan:

CURRENCY NEWS

The CFA franc, the currency of much of West and Central Africa, was devalued by 50% recently, producing extraordinary values for travelers to the region. Although the value of the currency was cut in half, prices have not yet risen to account for the change. This means that travelers are getting twice as many francs to the dollar, while paying the same or slightly more for goods and services than they were paying before devaluation.

The countries affected by the devaluation are Senegal, Cote d'Ivoire, Benin, Burkina Faso, Mali, Niger, Cameroon, Togo, Chad, Central Africa Republic, Gabon, and Congo. The governments of these countries have discouraged regional businesses, hotel, excursion companies, and transportation suppliers, as well as artisans and art dealers from raising their prices, in an

DESIGN TIPS

• To avoid orphans, try to gain a line in the first column so the text will flow upwards. Depending on the program you are using, you can do this several different ways. You may be able to track (see TRACKING, page 168) the type so it reflows; you can adjust the leading; you can add to the column length or width (if this does not disturb the general design of your project); or if all else fails, you can edit the text.

**See WIDOWS, page 183
to learn more about orphans.**

Output

Output is what comes out of your computer, (usually off your hard drive) in order to be represented by another device.

You can output to many different devices and in different media. Some of the forms output can take:

- Paper
- Film
- Slides
- Fax
- Printing Plates
- Envelopes
- Video signals
- Overhead Transparencies
- Postscript files or any kind of file printed to a disk.

Output can be color, black and white or positive or negative, depending on what you are using it for.

Some of the common output devices in desktop publishing are imagesetters, laser printers, dot matrix printers, film recorders, and video editing equipment.

DEMONSTRATION

Here are some examples of output devices:

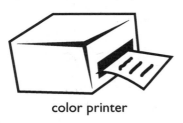

color printer

desktop printer

Page Numbers

Page numbers are a part of your document and should be considered a part of your design.

Page numbers should be easy to locate and read at a glance. They can appear in any part of your document, as long as they consistently appear in the same position (on the left and right pages).

DESIGN TIPS

With a little effort, your page numbers can be an interesting part of your design. Here are some of the things you can do to make your page numbers more lively and attractive: box them, put them in bars, reverse them add a tint or shade, or actually spell out the number.

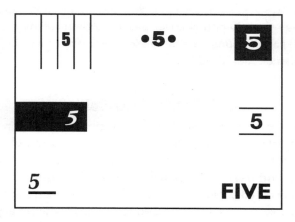

Paper

❑

Paper used in desktop publishing and printing comes in several standard sizes and in many different qualities and finishes.

SIZES AND WEIGHT

These are the common sizes in desktop publishing:

- **Letter:** 8 ½" x 11"
- **Legal:** 8½" x 14"
- **Tabloid:** 11" x 17"

These sizes, along with larger sheet sizes, are standard in North America. In other parts of the world, paper is measured in ISO (International Organization for Standardization) sizes. Paper is referred to by its *basis weight*. This is the weight, measured in pounds, of 500 sheets of a particular type paper cut to its *basic size*. In the United States, different grades of paper — *cover, text, ledger, and newsprint* for example — all have different standard sheet sizes, (which is why 100 pound text paper is *lighter* than 80 pound cover paper). When talking about paper, pounds is abbreviated by #. Paper weight can also be measured in grams.

TYPES OF PAPER

There are many different kinds of paper, which come in a variety of finishes (degree of smoothness and texture). Here are some of the categories of paper:

- **Bond** Also called *writing* or *ledger*. This is basic uncoated paper used in most desktop printers and copiers as well as for stationery. Paper without any particular texture is called *vellum* or *wove*. Some of the common textures in writing paper are *laid* (paper with a striped texture) and *linen* finishes.

- **Uncoated Offset** Also called *uncoated* or *text.* This is uncoated paper for use in offset lithography. Uncoated paper is not glossy or smooth, like coated paper; it is usually used for paper in a booklet, newsletters or similar publication.

- **Coated Offset** also called just *coated.* Coated paper has a smooth glossy finish. Brochures, catalogs and newsletters printed on coated paper often have a slicker, more upscale look than if printed on uncoated paper. Four color printing is usually done on coated paper.

- **Cover** Cover paper is heavier than text or offset. It is usedfor booklet covers, brochures, and to make presentation folders. Cover paper is often textured and in color. There are hundreds of different types of cover stocks, and they are often manufactured to match a corresponding text weight paper.

- **Newsprint** This is the light, pulpy stock used for newspapers.

- **Index.** This is heavier paper that comes with a smooth finish, in several standard colors. It is sturdy paper that is less expensive than cover stock.

Printing

Printing, in the most general sense, is the process of transferring an original image to paper (or some other surface) in order to make multiple copies.

The first printing method desktop publishers usually encounter is their office or desktop printer. In this case, the original image is an original file (see PRINTING (DESKTOP), page 113).

Beyond the office, however, are many other printing methods, most of which use a printing press to distribute ink on paper. The vast majority of printed work is reproduced using one of these methods.

WHY PRINT?

There many reasons why commercial artists and graphic designers use professional printers to reproduce their work. Here are a few of the most important reasons:

Quantity. Beyond a few hundred copies, a desktop printer is an inefficient way to generate large quantities of pages. A printing press is designed to produce thousands, even millions of high-quality reproductions.

Cost. Because printing presses are designed to produce large quantities, the cost per unit drops substantially, the more pieces you print. Offset printing is an extremely efficient way to reproduce artwork.

Color. Color printing on the desktop is still fairly expensive per copy, though it is a great way to reproduce color pages in small quantities. Color printouts are not usually as good quality as professionally printed color work and are only suitable for certain projects. Also, you can generally control the color quality of professional printing much more than you can desktop printing.

Complex documents. Your desktop printer produces pages only in selected sizes, and it only prints on papers of a limited weights. Furthermore, when it comes to folding, perforating, and cutting, desktop printers have limited capabilities.

Finishing. A print shop not only provides the service of reproducing your document; it also folds, collates, trims, assembles and packs your printed piece.

PRINTING OPTIONS

If you decide to take your job to a professional printer, you will have to select the kind of printing method most suitable for your project. A quick look in the local yellow pages demonstrates how many choices you have. Below are some of the most common printing choices, with their common uses.

Offset Lithography (Planographic Printing)

Most printing today is done by offset lithography. This is an inexpensive method of printing where ink is transferred onto paper using a plate made of plastic, paper or metal. Lithography uses the basic principle that oil and water don't mix; printing plates in offset lithography have surfaces that either attract or repel ink according to the image area. The image areas are inked and printed to a rubber blanket, and are then offset or transferred to paper thus creating an impression. Some offset presses can print thousands of impressions a minute.

Small print shops can usually have offset presses that print in one or two colors. Larger print shops offer four color printing (or more).

Newsletters, brochures, direct mail, and publications are printed offset. Most stationery, business cards, envelopes and mailing labels are printed offset, as are most books and magazines.

Continued

Relief Printing

In relief printing, image areas are raised above the surface of the plate and ink is transferred from this surface to the printing surface. The most common method of relief printing is flexography, which uses a rubber or soft plastic plate.

Flexography is used for industrial printing, like cartons, paper products (tissues and gift wrap paper), packaging and labels. Flexography is used for printing onto varied surfaces such as plastic, acetate, corrugated cardboard, cellophane or foil.

Wood block printing, and letterpress printing — some of the oldest forms of printing — are also methods of relief printing.

Intaglio

In intaglio methods of printing, the image area is lower than the surface of the plate. Ink fills these areas and then, with pressure, is transferred to paper. Intaglio plates are made either chemically, by machine, or by hand. Engraving and gravure are examples of intaglio printing methods, as is etching.

Engraving is often used for fine, high-quality printing in small runs. Wedding invitations, and occasionally, business cards and stationery, are engraved. Gravure printing is used for postage stamps, magazine supplements, and stock certificates.

Screen printing

This printing method uses porous fabric which allows ink to flow through areas not covered by a stencil. Screen printing lends itself to particularly bright colors. Screen printing, also called *silk screening* can be used to print on almost any surface. Screen printing is used for printing signs, billboards, decals, wallpaper, glass bottles, and posters among other things. It is also used for printing fabric; tee shirts, caps, bags, and banners are usually printed by screen printing.

A few other printing methods you may encounter:

Embossing
A type of relief method that actually presses an image into the surface of paper, in this way creating a raised impression.

Die-cut
A method of using razor-sharp steel rules which have been customized to cut unique forms and outlines from printed sheets.

Thermography
Also called *raised lettering*. A kind of effect often used on business cards that gives the look of enamel finished, raised letters.

DEMONSTRATION

Below is an illustration that shows the principle behind the different printing methods.

Offset   Relief

Intaglio   Screen

Continued

DESIGN TIPS

- Printing is a complex profession in and of itself, with its own rules and principles. Do not assume that because you made a document and printed it on your office printer, that it is suitable or ready for professional printing. If you want to have something printed professionally, review the job with your printer *before* you deliver it. This is also true if you are planning to deliver a floppy disk to the printer. Discuss color, size, paper, schedule, delivery method and cost before you get too far into the job.

- Just as you have the responsibility to deliver a professionally prepared piece of artwork to your printer, the printer has the responsibility to deliver the job you specified to you. If you ordered a certain color or paper, that is what you should get. Put your order in writing by using a purchase order. Be specific, and make sure you get what you ordered.

**See PRINTING (DESKTOP), page 113,
COLOR OFFSET PRINTING, page 28
to learn more about printing.**

Printing (Desktop)

When you finish your desktop publishing file, the most common way to output your file is by printing it. (See OUTPUT, page 104)

You can print your document to any one of many devices. Some of the common types of black and white printers are:

- **Laser**
- **Dot matrix**
- **Ink jet**
- **Plotter**
- **Daisy wheel**
- ***High Resolution Imagesetter (Linotronic, Varityper or Agfa).**

*NOTE: These are high resolution prepress devices, not devices for proofing your work.

You can also print your file to a color device, if one is available. There are many different kinds of color printers that use a variety different technologies. Some of the more common types of color desktop printers are:

- **Ink jet (Iris, HP)**
- **Dye sublimation (4CAST, 3M)**
- **Thermal dye transfer (QMS, Tektronix)**
- **Laser (Cannon)**

Besides these devices, you can print your file to film recorders, video recorders, or to another disk (as a print file or PostScript file).

Continued

DESKTOP PRINTING BASICS

In order to print your document, your computer needs to send or download the data contained in your file to your printer. If your printer has been installed correctly, your program will recognize and be able to communicate with it. If not, your computer will not be able to find the printer in order to send it the necessary information.

When your computer transfers information to your printer, it isn't just sending text; it sends information about the appearance of your file. This formatting information includes the typefaces in the document, the size of the page, the margins, the number of pages, and anything else that describes your document. The more information contained in your document — the more fonts and graphics you used — the longer your page will take to print. This is because each typeface has its own unique characteristics that need to be described and downloaded to the printer as part of the printing instructions.

There may be occasions when you try to print a document and nothing happens (or you get an error message). You may have created a document that is simply too big for your printer to handle. Graphics, in particular, can exponentially increase the complexity of your document. Because of this, most programs allow you to print your document in a *draft mode*. A *draft mode* prints your document without graphics, or in some cases (depending on the program) lets you print with graphics rendered in a rough (not finely drawn) form. Printing in a *draft mode* can significantly speed up printing.

The information your computer sends to your printer is encoded in a language that tells the printer how to draw your page. Laser printers use two main page description codes: *bitmap* and *PostScript®*.

Bitmap laser printers draw type and pages by mapping artwork to a grid pattern of pixels. The pixels are either on (black) or off (white), which is then represented visually as black or white.

PostScript® is a sophisticated page description language. It allows precision and flexibility in drawing type and graphics. PostScript® uses mathematical calculations to draw type and graphics. To use PostScript®, you must have a printer with a PostScript® interpreter. Note that not all printing devices read PostScript®.

Fonts are either usually either bitmap, PostScript® or TrueType®. Clip art is usually PostScript® (called *EPS* or *Encapsulated PostScript*) or bitmap clip art. You need a postscript printer to print EPS art. PostScript® art is usually better quality than bitmap art, but you only get the benefits of PostScript® art if you are printing to a PostScript® printer.

RESOLUTION OR DPI

Resolution or sharpness of your output — the amount of detail it contains — is measured in dots per inch (dpi). The more dots per inch your printer can produce, the better the quality of your printout. Most dot matrix printers have a resolution of 150 dpi to 360 dpi. Most common laser printers have a resolution of 300 dpi. Better laser printers have a resolution of 600 dpi to 1200 dpi. High resolution printers, the kind used in large art departments, design studios and service bureaus (see SERVICE BUREAU, page 145) output files at resolutions, from 900 dpi to 4000 dpi.

PRINTING OPTIONS

Most programs come with at least one dialog box, often called *Print Setup* or *Page Setup* that allows you to make choices regarding the file you plan to print. These dialog boxes provide you with choices as basic as page size, ori-

Continued

entation, range of pages to print, number of copies, and whether pages should be collated or not. Most programs give additional printing options, such as whether to print in a draft mode, in reverse (negative), with hidden text or annotations included, in reverse page order and more.

COMPUTER TIPS

• If you are printing a file with linked graphics — graphics imported into your file but not included or embedded within the file itself — you must make the linked graphic file available when you go to print. For example, if you give a disk to someone with a file you created and that file has imported graphics, make sure you include the graphic files on the disk as well.

The same thing is true for fonts. If you created a file with certain fonts, those fonts must be available to the computer system used to print the document when you or someone else attempts to print the file. If your printer cannot find the fonts originally used, it will substitute them with other fonts (or in some cases, draw a coarse approximation of your typeface). This is why most Print Setup dialog boxes have a selection referring to *Default Fonts*. Default fonts are what your printer uses when it can't find the original typefaces used in your document. When you send a job to a service bureau (a professional output service) make sure you send them your fonts and graphics.

Post script fonts always have two parts — a screen font and a printer font. Make sure that you send both parts to your service bureau.

See RESOLUTION, page 122, HALFTONE, page 66 to learn more about desktop printing.

Proofing

Proofing is the act of checking your work — a vital step in every desktop publishing project.

Each time you print out a version of your document, you need to proof it for both copy and style errors. The purpose of proofing is to save yourself costly and embarrassing mistakes; you don't want to wait until you print 10,000 leaflets to find you spelled the client's name incorrectly or printed the wrong date for an event.

When you proof, use a hard copy (see HARD COPY, page 68.) printout of your document. No matter how many times you review a document on the screen, it is not the same as reading a clean, printed version of your file.

As you read, mark corrections on your hard copy (see PROOFREADING MARKS, page 119.). Then, check off corrections as you make them to your computer document. Always keep this *draft* or *proof* for later reference.

DEMONSTRATION

Here's an example of a postcard that needs proofing.

Henry Hawthorne College — *Word repeats!*

invites you to a showing

of paitings by by artist — *Spelling*

AMANDA RILROTH

Tuesday, January 27, 1996

6 pm to 8 pm — *Correct time is 7 to 9*

Wentworth H**all** — *Should be regular not bold*

(212)555-5382 for more information

Wrong Number! Change to 5383

Is there enough room for labels?

Continued

DESIGN TIPS

- Make a checklist to keep handy and use every time you need to proof an important document. Run down the list and review everything item-by-item. Here's a sample of what to include on your checklist:

  ✓ **Names — Did you spell them correctly?**

  ✓ **Phone numbers — Check area codes too.**

  ✓ **Addresses — Check all numbers and names.**

  ✓ **Dates — Are they accurate?**

  ✓ **Spelling— Check every word line-by-line and *don't rely on a spell checker.* Spell checkers don't check for meaning. (Don't forget to check the headline.)**

  ✓ **Hyphenations—Watch for strange breaks.**

  ✓ **Widows and orphans — Watch for these.**

  ✓ **Captions — Are they correct?**

  ✓ **Typestyle — Did you use the correct type-styles and fonts throughout your documents? Are your headings consistent in size? Style errors are difficult to catch on the screen — it's best to use a printed proof.**

  ✓ **Missing copy — Read the copy through for content. Did you accidentally delete copy somewhere?**

  ✓ **Print preparation — Is your document fin-ished correctly? Are fold marks in the right place? Is your document the correct size? Do you have all your pages?**

  ✓ **Finally — don't forget to check everything: including page numbers, headers, footers, etc.**

  Check your document against your original manuscript. Proof carefully to save yourself costly mistakes!

Proofreading Marks

spelligh

Proofreading marks are a set of standard symbols that indicate corrections on a document.

If you use proofreading marks to correct or "mark up" your copy, you are guaranteed that editors, writers, printers, desktop publishers and typesetters will understand them. This is important in an office where several people may work on one document.

Use the following proofreading marks on a hard copy version of your document. *Always mark your copy with a color pen that stands out from the document itself.* Otherwise you may not see them when you sit down at your computer to make corrections.

Keep your corrected proof. It is a good way to keep track of the work you have done on a document, and you may need it for reference later.

The traditional way to proof is to make double notation of your corrections. Mark your change directly on the text (as done below), then note it again in the margin next to the line where the correction appears.

STYLE CORRECTIONS:

bf	Set type bold
ital	Set type italic
caps	Set type uppercase
lc	Set type LOWERCASE
caps/lc	Set type upper and lowercase
rom	Set type roman
sc	Set type small caps

Continued

119

PROOFREADING MARKS

SPACING AND POSITION CORRECTIONS:

#	Add space
⌒	Close up space
eg #	Equalize space in a line
[	[Move left
]	Move right]
ctr.	Center a line
ℓ	Delete a word, letter, phrase
stet	Let it stand (ignore correction)
(sp)	Spell out (don't abbrev.)
⌐	Break line here (send to next line)
¶	Start a new paragraph here. ¶
run in	Remove a paragraph and bring line up
tr	Transpose words (places switch)

PUNCTUATION

⊙	Put a period here
˄	Put a comma here
˅	Put an apostrophe here
=	Add a hyphen
(/)	Add parentheses here
!/	Add an exclamation mark
?/	Add a question mark
☐	Add an em space (indent)

**See PROOFING page 117,
for more about proofreading marks.**

Register Marks

These are the small symbols that allow a printer (in a print shop) to line up different layers of a piece of art precisely.

Artwork might have layers, for example, if it is being printed in two colors; each color would be represented by a separate piece of film. The two colors must line up perfectly on the printing press so the colors will print in the proper position. The printer lines up layers of art by matching the register marks on one layer to the register marks on another layer.

DEMONSTRATION

This is a business card with (four) register marks.

Fitzgerald Planetarium

Galileo Klein
Director, Educational Programs

1818 Stargazer Way, New Holland, CA 90157

**See MECHANICAL, page 97
to learn more about register marks.**

Resolution

Resolution is a measure of a device's ability to reproduce detail.

Specifically, it is a measure of how much information a device uses to render an image within a given space, usually within an inch. Resolution will tell you how much detail you can expect from a certain device. But be warned — there are few terms in desktop publishing that can be used in such a range of contexts. All devices that render an image usually provide some information about resolution, and each device measures resolution differently.

Both input devices, like scanners, and output devices, like printers, use resolution to describe how much detail they can reproduce.

- Laser printers measure resolution in dots per inch (dpi).

- Halftone screens measure resolution or *screen frequency* in lines per inch (lpi).

- Monitors measure resolution in pixels per inch (ppi).

- Scanners measure resolution in dots per inch (dpi), pixels per inch (ppi), or occasionally, samples per inch, depending on the term the manufacturer has chosen to use.

The one principle common to all measures of resolution is this; the more units per inch (the higher the number), the more detail and precision you will get in reproducing your image. A 300 dpi printer produces output that is not as a sharp as a 600 dpi printer, which in turn is not as sharp as a 1200 dpi printer. Devices are often referred to as *low resolution* or *high resolution,* depending on the number of dots per inch they reproduce.

DEMONSTRATION

To better understand the concept of resolution, let's take a closer look at the most common expression of resolution — dots per inch. Below are examples of different amounts of dots per inch:

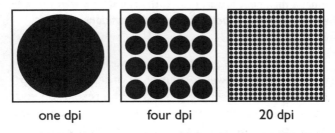

one dpi   four dpi   20 dpi

This is scanned at 50 dpi.   This is scanned at 200 dpi.

The more dots per inch the more detail your image will contain. But remember — *when it comes to graphics, higher resolution only matters if you are outputting to a device that can represent the detail.* Every device has a limit to how much detail it is physically able to reproduce.

For example, there is no point in scanning an image at 200 dpi if you are only going to use it for display purposes on a 72 dpi monitor.

The higher the resolution you use in scanning, the larger your file size will be.

Continued

COMPUTER TIPS

- Although it may be confusing at times, be aware that sometimes the resolution of one device affects the resolution of another. For example, a printer with a *low* resolution (300 dpi) cannot print a halftone screen with a *high* resolution (133 lpi). *The device with the lowest resolution is usually the main determinant of image quality.*

- Some applications give users the option of outputting documents at a *lower* resolution in order to speed up printing. This is because the higher the resolution you use in printing, the more data your printing device has to process. For simple proofing, a lot of detail isn't always necessary.

- *Resolution has nothing to do with color.* In computer terms, color is measured by *bit depth* — how many bits per pixel your file contains.

See PRINTING, page 108, HALFTONE, page 66, and SCANNING, page 135 to learn more about resolution.

Retouching

Retouching refers to changes made to the appearance of a photographic image.

In the context of desktop publishing, there are many software programs that supply the tools for electronic (or digital) retouching. These applications allow users to retouch an image, then use the image as a graphic in their desktop publishing files.

Images are retouched for many different reasons:

- To remove a stain, smudge or other damage.
- To improve image quality by lightening or darkening the picture, or by changing the contrast.
- To change colors.
- To create special effects like silhouettes, vignettes, and ghosted images.
- To actually change the image itself! Electronic retouching provides extraordinary tools to transform and manipulate an image.

DEMONSTRATION

This is an example of the power of electronic retouching:

Before

After

Continued

RETOUCHING

Retouching lets users perform photographic magic. Here we took two photographs and combined them using Adobe Photoshop® to make a third, totally new image:

Here are examples of other special effects you can create with electronic retouching (or with traditional photographic retouching):

Above is an example of a *silhouetted* photo (see SILHOUETTE, page 152).

Left is an example of a *vignette*. The edges have been softened so that they fade to the background.

COMPUTER TIPS

- If you plan to try your hand at electronic retouching, keep in mind that you need solid computer power behind you! Photos tend to be big files, and color image files are gigantic. A 4"x 5" color photo scanned at 300 dpi (see RESOLUTION, page 122) can take up eight or ten megabytes of space. If you plan to retouch that image, you will need several times more empty space on your hard drive, as well as plenty of memory.

- If you want to experiment with electronic retouching, start off with a low resolution scan, 72 dpi for example. Although it won't be of suitable printing quality, your computer will be able to handle the file as you practice and experiment.

Reverse

A reverse is when type or a symbol appears in white against a black (or color) background.

Normally, we view type the other way around — black against a white background. In graphic design, a common way to break up the monotony of text-heavy pages is to reverse type from a black background, thus adding a graphic element.

DEMONSTRATION

These are examples of type reversed out of bars:

About our frequent flyer program

turn to page 24

This is a logo reversed out of a box:

This is an illustration that has been reversed:

128

DESIGN TIPS

- Try reversing only one letter to create an interesting initial cap.

> **F** or over 75 years, Smedley's Department Store has been a fixture on the corner of Franklin and Mercer Avenues. Now all that is about to change.

- The printing term for reverse is *knock-out*. This is when type or a logo is literally removed (or knocked-out) from the background.

- You can reverse call outs, headers, page numbers, and almost anything else you can think of.

ENERGY *SAVINGS*

Fitzgerald Planetarium

N E W S L I N E

W E L C O M E

By Veronica Jordan

Rule

A rule is the graphic design term for a *line*.

In graphic design, a rule is used for both function and decoration. You can use a rule to:

- Separate columns.

- Give definition to the shape of a page by using one at the top and bottom.

- Separate or offset areas within text.

- Add a border to a graphic.

- Separate a header or footer from the rest of the copy.

- Offset titles or headings.

The size or weight of a rule is generally measured in points, although some word processing programs measure rules in inches. The thinnest printable rule — usually $1/4$ of a point thick — is called a *hairline rule*.

DEMONSTRATION

Here are examples of various horizontal rules, measured in points:

————————————————	hairline (.25pt)
————————————————	.5 pt.
————————————————	1 pt.
————————————————	2 pt.
————————————————	3 pt.
————————————————	4 pt.
————————————————	5 pt.
————————————————	6 pt.
————————————————	8 pt.

Here are examples of rules, measured in inches:

――――――――――――――――	.005"
――――――――――――――――	.01"
――――――――――――――――	.02"
――――――――――――――――	.03"
――――――――――――――――	.04"
――――――――――――――――	.06"
――――――――――――――――	.08"
――――――――――――――――	.1"
――――――――――――――――	.15"

DESIGN TIPS

• Rules don't have to be solid lines. They can be dotted, dashed, or double lines; they can be thick or thin:

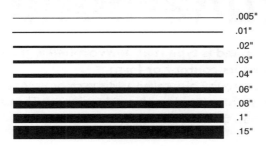

Runaround

A runaround is type that flows around a graphic, following its contour or form.

A runaround, also called a *type wrap* or *wraparound,* is an effect often used in ads and brochures. The user selects how far to offset the type from the graphic.

DEMONSTRATION

Below is an example of a runaround:

The famous resort of Cervina is set amid magnificent scenery in the Aosta Valley on the Southside of the Matterhorn. The skiing is superb for everyone, from beginner upwards; intermediate skiers in particular have a marvelous time tackling the long open runs which are well above the tree line and go on without interruption for miles. Experienced skiers will find very good off trail snow skiing at Cervinia.

DESIGN TIPS

- Try putting a graphic between two columns so that type wraps to the left and the right of the graphic:

Deep sea fishing is a sport that inspires tremendous loyalty. For those who cannot understand why any person would want to spend eight hours in the hot sun trailing an elusive fish, a deep sea fisherman would spare few words. Fishing needs no explanation according to those who build their whole year around the one week when they take their gear out to the middle of the Atlantic for a week of communion with fish. "We do it because

Scaling

When you scale an object in desktop publishing, you change it's size.

The word scaling implies that an object is enlarged or reduced on two dimensions — the horizontal (x-axis) and the vertical (y-axis). The computer makes a calculation every time it scales an object, and proportionally enlarges along these two dimensions.

Some programs let you scale an object in only one dimension, or along only one axis. In this case, you are scaling either horizontally or vertically.

DEMONSTRATION

This is type that has been scaled. The shape of the letter remains proportional as the size increases:

This is a graphic that has been scaled:

Continued

DESIGN TIPS

- Scaling on one dimension can give you some interesting special effects.

Normal Photo   Horizontally scaled
only

Normal Photo

Vertically scaled only

**See SIZE, page 154
to learn more about scaling.**

Scanning

Scanning is the process of digitizing photos and graphics, using a device called a *scanner*.

A scanner converts pictures into pieces of electronic information that can then be read by your computer and displayed on your monitor.

Put even more simply, scanners lets you bring photos and graphics inside your computer.

Scanning can be also be used to input text with the help of optical character recognition (OCR) software. OCR software recognizes characters as text, and converts scanned pages into text files that can then be treated like any other text file.

There are many types of scanners:

- **Flatbed scanners**
- **Hand-held scanners**
- **Slide scanners**
- **Drum scanners**
- **Digital cameras**

Each scanner has different capabilities and can interpret images with different degrees of precision.

Once an image has been scanned into your computer, it becomes data, just like any other file. A scanned file is *not* a photo inside your computer.

DEMONSTRATION

Below is are examples of art that has been scanned:

This is line art.

This is grayscale.

Continued

COMPUTER TIPS

- Many people have trouble understanding that while you can scan almost anything, you can't scan *everything* the same way. Your scanner has different *scanning modes*; the mode you choose depends on the nature of your original artwork (ie. is it a photo or a drawing). It also depends on the ultimate use of your scan (ie. how it will be printed).

  Since there are many issues that go into a scan — input, output, and even the type of computer and program you are using — it is not uncommon to be confused by options in scanning. Furthermore, different manufacturers use different terms to refer to the same thing. As you use your equipment and software, you will become more familiar with its capabilities, and with the optimum conditions for various types of scans. Here are a few guidelines that will help you make sense out of scanning;

WHAT ARE YOU INPUTTING?

Is your scan a line drawing? Is it a photograph? Or is it a picture that has already been printed in a magazine? Is it color or black and white? Each one of these options requires a different scanning mode or setting. The list below will help you select the corresponding setting for the type of art you are using. We have tried to include the different terms you are likely to encounter.
Note: In the world of high-end scanning, color is referred to as Bit Depth. This is the number of "bits" of information per pixel.

LINE DRAWING　　This is a drawing that is made of only two colors, usually black and white. The scanner only needs to interpret what areas are black, and what areas are white to get an accurate representation. **Scanning mode: one bit; also called bitmap, monochrome, bi-level.**

GRAYSCALE

This is artwork that has many shades of gray that blend together. Another word for this kind of artwork is *continuous tone* or *halftone*. A photograph is an example of grayscale art. When you scan this kind of artwork, you want to retain as much information as you can about the various shades of gray. Most scanners can recognize 256 shades of gray, which is called *256 grayscale*. There is also grayscale scanning that produces 16, 32, and 64 levels of gray.
Scanning mode: 8 bit; also called 4 bit, grayscale, photo.

PRINTED PHOTO

If you are scanning a photo that has already been printed, you may run into trouble; when you scan a photo that has already been printed as a halftone (see HALFTONE page 66) you run the risk of getting a *moiré pattern* — a distracting pattern that runs through your artwork (see MOIRÉ, page 100). This is hard to avoid, but if it happens, try scanning your photo at a different angle, use a different scanning resolution, or scan your photo at a different size.
Scanning mode: same as for grayscale or color photo.

COLOR PHOTO

If you are scanning a color photo and you want it in black and white, you can scan it as grayscale. It will then be treated like a black and white photo. If you plan to print your photo from your computer to a color printer, you need to scan it in color. Color scanning produces very large files compared to other kinds of scanning.
Scanning Settings: 24 bit, also called color, 8 bit.

Continued

SCANNING

For each of the above modes, you will need to choose a setting that tells the scanner how many dots per inch (dpi) you wish to use to scan your image (see RESOLUTION, page 122.). The higher the setting, the more detail you will obtain in your image. (This doesn't mean that you will see more detail when you print your file — see DESIGN TIPS below. Also, the higher the dpi setting, the larger your file will be.

If you are scanning *line art*, use a setting that corresponds to the resolution of your printer. For example, a piece of line art should be scanned at 300 dpi, if it is to be output to 300 dpi.

If you are scanning a *halftone* or *color picture* that will be printed to a device that uses a halftone-based printing method, such as a desktop printer or an imagesetter, scan your image at *twice* your halftone screen frequency (lpi). If you don't know what your halftone screen is, scan your image at 300 dpi — that is usually high enough for any use.

If you are scanning artwork for use in a monitor display (such as a presentation) scan your artwork at 72 dpi.

This is an example of grayscale art scanned with only six levels of gray. This kind of art is called *posterized*.

WHAT ARE YOU OUTPUTTING?

Scanners also let you supply information about the way the file will be printing out. Your scanning software will let you select the final size of your picture or graphic; in other words, it will scale your image as it scans. Most scanners also provide a preview option so you can select the specific area you wish to scan.

Scanners also allow you to select a particular file format for your scan (see FILE FORMATS, page 47) when you save it. TIFF, EPS, BITMAP, and PICT, are examples of file formats. You need to make sure you save your document in a format that can be read by your program of choice.

DESIGN TIPS

- Scanning is an art in itself. We have reviewed only the basics that are part of every scan. There are many other features that can be part of the scanning process, such as contrast, sharpening, gamma and more. Be sure to read the documentation and manual that came with your scanner to gain a full understanding of how your scanner works.

- Keep track of the settings you have used in your scanning. Keep a log or reference book of your scan results. Note what works and what doesn't, and eventually you will have concrete information as to how to get the best possible scans with your scanning device.

- Higher resolution does not always mean you will get better printed results. You can only print as much as your printer can handle. Any information beyond that is irrelevant. For example, below we have three different scans of a lion. Because this book is printed at 85 lpi, there is be no visible difference between a picture scanned at 200 dpi and the ones scanned at 300 and

Continued

600 dpi. Though there is more information in the files that were scanned at a higher resolution, the printer can't reproduce that much detail. Notice how much larger the files become as resolution increases.

200 dpi (384k)   300 dpi (864k)   400 dpi (1.5 Meg)

- Some scanners may allow you to select a *color mode*. A color mode refers to the way your file represents color information. Examples of color modes are CMYK, RGB, and GRAYSCALE.

**See FILE FORMAT, page 47, GRAPHIC, page 56,
RETOUCHING, page 125, and
HALFTONE, page 66
to learn more about scanning.**

Script

ABC

Script refers to typefaces that mimic the look of stylized handwriting.

Script fonts are usually formal in style, although there are many scripts that are casual and informal. The letters of script typefaces appear to connect, as if the letters were written in one flowing stroke.

Script fonts are commonly used for invitations and announcements, or to give something a personal, handwritten look.

DEMONSTRATION

These are examples of script typefaces:

Brush Script

Charme

Linoscript

Kaufmann Bold

Flemish Script

Snell Roundhand

DESIGN TIPS

- Some script typefaces often have a very small x-height (see X-HEIGHT page 184). This means that the lowercase letters are proportionally small (relative to the uppercase letters). You have to use these scripts at larger sizes, for them to be comfortably readable.

Serifs

Serifs are the small strokes on the ends of letters.

If a font has these small strokes they are called *serif* typefaces. Typefaces without serifs are called *sans serif* typefaces — French for "without serifs."

Serif typefaces are the more traditional basis of type design. Their form, including the varying stroke weights, is meant to reflect handwriting. Some typefaces, such as Bodoni, Caslon and Garamond, date back many centuries. There are many different categories of serif typefaces — Egyptian, Modern, Transitional, and Oldstyle, for example — that each reflect distinct design features.

Some popular serif typefaces are *Times Roman, Goudy, Garamond, Palatino* and *Caslon*. Some of the more popular sans serif typefaces are *Helvetica (Swiss or Helios), Franklin Gothic, Futura* and *Univers*.

DEMONSTRATION

Serifs come in many different shapes:

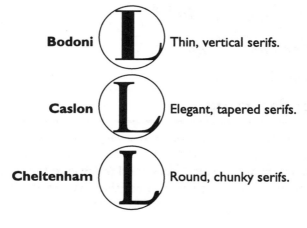

Bodoni — Thin, vertical serifs.

Caslon — Elegant, tapered serifs.

Cheltenham — Round, chunky serifs.

142

Memphis Blocky, rectangular serifs.

Below are some examples of sans serif type:

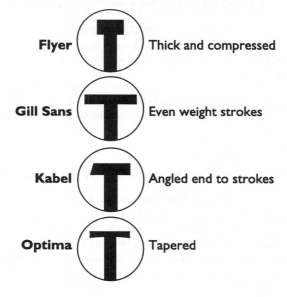

Flyer Thick and compressed

Gill Sans Even weight strokes

Kabel Angled end to strokes

Optima Tapered

DESIGN TIPS

• Studies have shown that serif type is considered more readable in large blocks, which is why books and newspapers are usually printed in a serif typeface.

• If you want to add a little variety to your design, use two typefaces — one serif and one sans serif. Assign each a different use. You might want to set all your main headings in the serif typeface, and all the subheadings and

Continued

body copy in the *sans serif* face. Or, try it the other way around. If you pick complementary, well-matched typefaces, you will find the use of two typefaces adds sophistication and interest to your design. *Make sure you pick typefaces with ample contrast.*

Here are two examples using Helvetica and Century:

Enjoy the Sights of Wilmont

There's so much to see!

Visitors to our area will have no trouble filling their days with all the fascinating sights of this historic region. You'll certainly want to start the day with a visit to the tulip gardens of Van Rijn Park where you'll see thousands of tulips, imported from Holland since the sixteenth century.

Then it's time for a visit to the Wilmont Clown Museum,

Continued on page 3

Enjoy the Sights of Wilmont

There's so much to see!

Visitors to our area will have no trouble filling their days with all the fascinating sights of this historic region. You'll certainly want to start the day with a visit to the tulip gardens of Van Rijn Park where you'll see thousands of tulips, imported from Holland since the sixteenth century.

Then it's time for a visit to the Wilmont Clown Museum,

Continued on page 3

**See TYPEFACE, page 171
to learn more about serif and sans serif type.**

Service Bureau

A service bureau is a place you go to obtain various computer-related services that are too expensive or difficult to perform in-house.

Service bureaus originated because much of the equipment involved in desktop publishing is extremely expensive. A piece of equipment like a high-end scanner can cost several hundreds of thousands of dollars. Service bureaus perform specific services at project-by-project rates.

The most common service supplied by service bureaus is providing high-quality output of your desktop publishing files. Service bureaus run your files or *image* your files to imagesetters that print out at very high resolution (see RESOLUTION, page 122). This output, called *linotronic output, repro* or *lino,* depending on the shop, is of a much higher quality and sharpness than you can get from most office printers. Professional desktop publishers and graphic designers rarely use anything less than high-resolution output for their work.

This is an example of some of the services a professional service bureau might supply:

- **Paper (called "RC", resin coated) and film output**
- **Color proofs and comps**
- **Scanning**
- **Retouching**
- **Film recorder (to print slides)**
- **File conversion**
- **Trapping and print preparation**

Continued

DEMONSTRATION

This is an example of the information you would to need provide to order paper output from a service bureau:

Turnaround (Check one):

Priority: _____ Rush: _____ Standard: _____

IMAGESETTING/OUTPUT

Filename	Program/version	Crop marks	# of pages	Page Size
_____	_____	y/n	_____	_____
_____	_____	y/n	_____	_____
_____	_____	y/n	_____	_____

☐ 1270 dpi ☐ 2540 dpi   Line Screen_____ (default is 85 lpi)

Special instructions: _____

_____

_____

Fonts Used: _____

_____

DESIGN TIPS

- When you send your files to a service bureau for output, you must specify exactly what you want.

  ### CHECKLIST FOR ORDERING REPRO:

  ✔ **Always keep a backup copy of your file. *Never* send your original file.**

  ✔ **Supply service bureau with unusual fonts (that your service bureau may not have).**

  ✔ **Specify the halftone screen you wish to use.**

  ✔ **Include all linked (imported) graphics.**

  ✔ **Clearly write your file name and the pages you wish to print on your order form.**

  ✔ **Tell your service bureau the name of the program used to create your file.**

Shade

Shade refers to the intensity of a color, measured in percentages of dots.

Another more traditional term for shade is *tint*. A color that has a shade or tint of 100% is a solid color. A black box filled with a shade of 90% black means that the color has been broken into a pattern of dots that will create a shade of dark gray. The lower the percentage, the lighter the shade.

Shading can be applied in various ways, depending on the power of your program. Some programs allow you to fill a box or a border with a shade. Others let you select shades or tints for type, and even apply tints to certain types of graphics.

DEMONSTRATION

These are examples of shades:

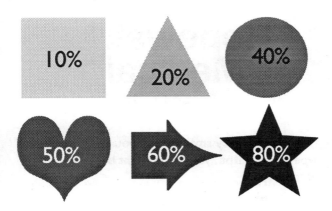

Continued

COMPUTER TIPS

- You may be able to apply shading in your program, but be aware that doesn't mean you can print out your document and be guaranteed good results. Your output device plays an important role in the quality of your final page. If you plan to use shades, and you are working in a more advanced program like QuarkXPress or Aldus PageMaker, it helps to understand the concept of halftone screen (see HALFTONE, page 66.). The halftone screen determines how sharply your shade will print.

DESIGN TIPS

- Shades add the illusion of color. If you want to add richness to a logo or to a busy page of type, introduce some shading.

- Never shade very small type. If you apply shades to type under 11 pt., your type might break up and be hard to read:

Ann Elk Interiors invites you to explore upholstery.

This is 8pt. Palatino regular, with a shade of 40%.

- Make sure you don't put black type against a shade or tint that is too dark. A good tint to use as a background is 20% or 30%:

Ann Elk Interiors invites you to explore upholstery.

Too dark!

This is 8pt. Palatino against a box with a shade of 65%.

Ann Elk Interiors invites you to explore upholstery.

Better

This is 8pt. Palatino against a box with a shade of 20%.

- You can use shading to call attention to certain blocks of information. For example, if you have an area in your design such as a table of contents, a masthead box, or a reminder, you can offset the information by adding a shade to the box.

**See HALFTONE, page 66
for more about shade.**

Sidebar

A sidebar is a boxed and separate block of copy that appears within a larger, longer story.

A sidebar is an element of editorial layout — the layout of stories or articles within a publication. A sidebar relates to the main story, but provides a slightly different point of view, or close-up, related to the main story. It is a diversion, a variation on the main theme that gives readers a break from long passages of text.

A sidebar often focuses on an individual who figures in the main story. A sidebar can also be a more in-depth review of an issue that arises in the main story only in passing. Or it can contain an informational or itemized list that relates to the story, as in the example below.

DEMONSTRATION

This is a side bar:

Small Businesses on the Move

Divide a page into columns. Copy appears here in your columns, flowing from the base of one column to the top of the next column. Your grid is a basis for your design. You can divide a page into columns many ways, combining them for a double column width when you choose. Copy appears here in your columns, flowing from the base of one column to the top of the next column. Your grid is a basis

Copy appears here in your columns, flowing from the base of one column to the top of the next column. Your grid is a basis for your design. You can divide a page into columns many ways, combining them for a double column width when you choose. Copy appears here in your columns, flowing from the base of one column to the top of the next column. Your grid is a basis for your design. You can

How to start your own business

Copy appears here in your columns, flowing from the base of one column to the top of the next column. Your grid is a basis for your design. You can divide a page into columns many ways, combining them for a double column width when you choose. Copy appears here in your columns, flowing from the base of one column to the top of the next column. Your grid is a

5

DESIGN TIPS

- A sidebar is often filled with a tint or color to offset it from the surrounding copy. You can also try a graduated tint (see BLEND, page 8.) for an attractive effect.

- A sidebar can run horizontally or vertically.

- You can even change the typeface of the type in the sidebar to something other than the main typeface to further offset the information.

Ron Rilroth; portrait of a success

Lorem ipsum dolor sit amet , consectetur adip iscing elit, sed diam nonumy eiusmod tempor incidunt ut labore et dolore magna aliquam erat volupat.

Ut einim as minim veniam, quis nostrud exercitation ull amcorpor suscipit laboris nisi ut aliquip ex ea commodo consequet .Lorem ipsum dolor sit amet , consectetur adip iscing elit, sed diam nonumy eiusmod tempor incidunt ut labore et dolore magna aliquam erat volupat.

Ut einim as minim veniam, quis nostrud exerci-

Ron Rilroth; portrait of a success

Lorem ipsum dolor sit amet , consectetur a-dip iscing elit, sed diam nonumy eius-mod tempor incidunt ut labore et dolore magna aliquam erat Ut einim as minim veniam, quis nostrud exercitation ull amcorpor suscipit laboris nisi ut aliquip

TIPS TO HELP YOU QUIT SMOKING NOW

1. Lorem ipsum dolor sit amet , consectetur adip
2. iscing elit, sed diam nonumy tempor incidunt ut labore et dolore magna aliquam erat volupat.
3. Ut einim as minim veniam, quis nostrud exercitation ull
4. Amcorpor suscipit laboris nisi ut aliquip ex ea commodo conse.
5. Est vel eum irure dolor.
6. In voluputate velit esse molestaie consequat, vel illum dolore eu fugiat nulla pariatur.
7. At vero eos et accusam et iousto odogio dignisaium qui blandit est praesent
8. Luptatum delenit aigue duos dolor et
9. Molestias excepteur sint occaecat cupidatat non provident, simil tempor
10. In culpa qui officia deserunt

Silhouette

A silhouette refers to a halftone (photograph) that has been outlined, with the background removed.

Traditionally, a silhouette is created by the printer's *prep department*. This is the place where a mechanical is brought to the next stage in (see MECHANICAL, page 97.) In computer graphics, a silhouette can be created using photo retouching software.

Use a silhouetted photo if you have a picture with an unattractive background, or if you want to show a product without background distractions.

DEMONSTRATION

This is an example of a silhouetting:

Before   After

DESIGN TIPS

- For a nice effect, try wrapping type around a silhouetted product photograph (if you have access to one, or if you know how to silhouette one yourself). This can give a very tasteful look to an ad or leaflet:

At Albright's, Natural Isn't Just a Trend

These days, with so much discussion about health and the environment, buying all-natural food is considered trendy is some circles. It isn't just a trend at Albright's. We've been selling all natural fruit and produce for over thirty years. And many of our customer's have been with us since the beginning; now that's commitment.

At Albright's we believe in the value of good health. If you're looking for a place where

good health is a way of life, come to Albright's, for the best in all-natural foods.

ALBRIGHT'S • 57 MAIN AVENUE • NEWTON

Size

Type size is expressed in points. The point size of a typeface is a measurement of the distance from the top of the ascender to the bottom of the descender.

Traditionally, type size is specified in standard sizes. Before computer typesetting, a printer could not possibly keep a font for every possible size. It was more practical to carry selected sizes: 6, 7, 8 ,9 10, 12, 14, 18, 24, 30, 36, 42, 48, 52, 60 and 72 point.

Today, the type size menu of most desktop publishing programs menus still offers these standard type sizes for convenience. However, usually you can also customize your menu or selection, and choose any type size you like.

You can format type in any size you wish, but if you are using bitmap fonts to print your document, you will only get acceptable results if you have a printer font for the type size you are printing. TrueType® and PostScript® font technologies can print type in any size.

DEMONSTRATION

This is 6 pt type

This is 7 pt. type.

This is 8 pt. type.

This is 9 pt. type.

This is 10 pt. type.

This is 11 pt. type.

This is 12 pt. type.

This is 14 pt. type.

This is 16 pt. type.

This is 20 pt. type.

This is 24 pt. type.

This is 30 pt. type.

This is 36 pt.

This is 42 pt.

This is 60

72 pt. = 1"

Continued

DESIGN TIPS

- If you are creating a document using different sizes of type, make sure you select sizes that are sufficiently different. Type that is only a point apart in size will not provide sufficient contrast. In this case, there is not enough difference between sizes to be visibly effective.

Marguerita's Gifts
announces their pre-holiday
SALE
Come in for special reductions on fine gift items.

Type sizes above are 10, 11 and 9 pts.

This is a more effective use of type size:

Marguerita's Gifts
announces their pre-holiday
SALE
Come in for special reductions on fine gift items.

Type sizes above are 12, 28 and 9 pts.

- For beginners, one of the first struggles is figuring out which type size to use for a project. Here are some guidelines to get you going. These suggestions are based on an 8 ½" x 11" page. They are only suggestions; there's no reason why copy can't be larger or smaller than suggested here, especially given the variety of projects you might be working on. Still, when in doubt, start with these sizes.

Suggested Type Sizes

Body copy: 9, 10 or 11 pt.
Subheadings: 12, 14 or 16 pt.
Headings: anywhere from 24 pt. and larger
Captions: 8 or 9 pt.

Here's how the recommended sizes might work:

About Our College of Nursing

Henry Hawthorne's program gives students more

On the following pages you will find everything you need to know about your new health bene-fits program. We know you'll be glad to hear about the improvements we've made to our coinsurance policy for hospitalization, our family coverage plan and our supplemental dental plan.

For over fifty years, we've been training healthcare professionals.

- When choosing a type size, keep in mind that different typefaces will have a larger or smaller appearance, even if they are supposed to be exactly the same size. This is because of the varying x-height of different typefaces (see X-HEIGHT, page 184).

Continued

SIZE

- Make sure you choose a type size that is appropriate for your readers. Menus should have large, easy to read type since the lighting is often low. Signs meant to be read from a distance also need to be large. Legal copy — the small lines of type that provide information required by law, can be small — 6 or 7 point. Select typefaces that are legible at the size you plan to use them; some typefaces are fine at larger sizes, but become difficult to read at smaller sizes.

See SCALING, page 133, BODY COPY, page 10 to learn more about size.

Small Caps

Small caps are capital letters approximately the size of lowercase letters (of the same size font).

Small caps are used instead of capital letters because they are less obtrusive. They are an attractive way of expressing acronyms and other words that need to be set in all capital letters. The abbreviations, AM, PM, A.D., and B.C. are usually set in small caps. Small caps also give an elegant and understated look to headings.

DEMONSTRATION

Below are examples of small caps:

7 AM TO 9 PM

COMMEMORATE THE HOLIDAY SEASON

ABOUT EAST SIDE AUCTIONEERS...

DESIGN TIPS

- You can use small caps in a "teaser" to introduce an article. Put your introduction to a story on the same line as the rest of the story, but set it in small caps.

  THERE'S NO BUSINESS LIKE SHOW BUSINESS. In New York City today, the stars of five major Broadway productions gathered for a salute to America's musical theater. The five casts performed highlights from their shows for a crowd that gathered in the heart of the theater district at lunch time today.

Special Characters

Special characters are type characters other than the standard letters, numbers, and basic punctuation usually included in a font.

There are many types of special characters. They include math fonts, accent marks, reference marks, monetary symbols and more. Another term for special characters are *pi fonts*.

Special characters might be included within a standard type font such as Helvetica, or they may be accessible only through a separate font. Many programs for desktop publishing systems come with a special font called *symbols* just for the purpose of supplying users with special characters.

DEMONSTRATION

These are examples some common special characters:

$$@ \# \% \pounds \cent \$ \infty \S \ddagger \P \neq \pm \div \geq \bullet$$

$$\text{›} \, ¤ \, ¿ \, \% \, ^\wedge \, ® \, © \, ^{TM} \, ` \, Æ \, ˘$$

$$\tau\rho\delta\alpha\beta\lambda\mu\pi\Delta E\Phi\Omega\Xi\Diamond\Upsilon$$

$$\aleph \, \daleth \, \rceil\!\!\!\Sigma \, \vee \Leftrightarrow \Leftarrow \Uparrow \Rightarrow \Downarrow$$

Stock Photography

Stock photography is photography that is supplied by *stock photo collections* — as opposed to photography that is commissioned.

To use stock photography, the user licenses (rents) a photo from a particular stock photo company for a specified purpose. The cost is less than hiring a photographer. The downside is that the image you rent can be used or licensed by other people after you have used it.

You can find almost any kind of picture in one of the many stock collections, from surfers to space shuttles. Themes include sports, travel, nature, business, industry, medicine, and much more. There are also stock collections available on CD-ROM — you can buy a quantity of reasonably priced, copyright-free images on one disk.

DEMONSTRATION

These are some examples of stock photography:

Style Sheets

HEADING
body copy
Caption

Style sheets, also called *styles*, are sets of formatting instructions that you define *yourself*, and then apply to your text. Styles automate the process of formatting by letting you apply a group of formatting commands in one step.

Styles are a powerful part of desktop publishing. If you create a lot of documents, long documents, recurring projects like newsletters, or if you have a style of copy that appears in different places throughout your documents, consider using style sheets. A simple user-defined set of styles might include a style for a heading, subheading, body copy and captions.

Most word processing programs let you create a set of styles that include formatting information about typeface, size, leading, alignment, tabs, and information. More advanced programs, like QuarkXPress and Aldus PageMaker let you include color, rules, hanging indents, tracking information and more.

One of the best things about style sheets is that they let you make overall changes to your document in one easy step. If you change an aspect of one of your styles, all the text that was created with that style will change automatically.

DEMONSTRATION

This is a dialog box showing a QuarkXPress style sheet
for a newsletter:

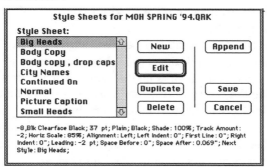

This is a dialog box showing a Microsoft® Word for
Windows™ style sheet:

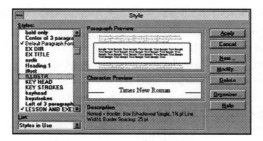

This is a dialog box showing a WordPerfect® style sheet:

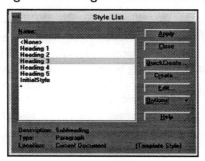

Tabs

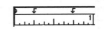

Tabs let you inset text and align rows of information automatically.

By pressing the tab key, text will align at a pre-selected point. In desktop publishing, a user can create multiple tab settings on a line or within a story, thus customizing the tab settings. Tabs are a very powerful tool for quick formatting, particularly for tables.

In some programs, tabs are indicated by tick marks or angled symbols. In other programs, tab stops are indicated by arrows, as in the example below.

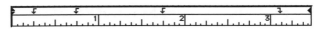

There are four basic tab settings: *left-aligned, right-aligned, center* and *decimal*. Each of these options will align information on the selected tab stop as shown below. Some programs let you include other types of tabs, such as comma tabs or customized tabs.

DEMONSTRATION

Below are examples of different tab alignments.

Left	Center	Right	Decimal
cauliflower	cauliflower	cauliflower	$17.95
celery	celery	celery	$9.22
string beans	string beans	string beans	$12.85
egg plant	egg plant	egg plant	$14.86
onions	onions	onions	$8.35
spinach	spinach	spinach	$1.32

DESIGN TIPS

- Use tabs to create address forms and return coupons by setting tabs with an underscore. Most programs will let you insert a *fill character* (a character that will fill the length of your tab when applied) when you create your tab. Some programs call this a *tab leader*. In the example below, lines are created by tabs with an underscore.

Name _____

Address _____

City _____**State** _____**Zip** _____

Phone _____ **Fax** _____

See DOT LEADER, page 44
to learn more about tabs.

Talent

Talent is something you develop over time, no matter how much you have to start with.

Whether you believe you have a lot of ability or very little, when it comes to visual art most people can improve their skills every day just by observation. All around you are opportunities to study graphic design. You'll find that as you raise your awareness of graphic design techniques, your own work will improve.

DESIGN TIPS

Below is a checklist of ways you can develop your skills just by daily observation.

✔ **When you read a newspaper or magazine, or open the mail, if something catches your eye take a moment to figure out why it got your attention. Was it an appealing typeface? A photo? A dramatic layout?**

✔ **If you see something you like, *save it*. Start a file of design samples. When it's time for you to design something, flip through your file and look for interesting design effects and uses of type that you can try in your own work.**

✔ **Study how different people solved design problems. Look at brochures, posters, and the business cards people give you. Take a moment to analyze them.**

✔ **Pay more attention to color and type. Do you see any trends in color use? In type use? Develop your powers of recognition.**

Thumbnail

A thumbnail sketch is a tiny, rough sketch that a graphic designer creates in order to explore layout and design ideas.

The point of doing a thumbnail sketch is that they are a quick and simple way to work out visual concepts and you can do a lot of them in a short time.

DEMONSTRATION

These are thumbnail sketches for a letterhead (stationery.)

This is the logo that we are working with in the thumbnails.

DESIGN TIPS

- Thumbnails let you work with basic elements: headings, columns of type, graphics and logos, for example. Use thumbnails for laying out these basic elements, and concern yourself with details in either a full-size layout or at the computer.

**See LAYOUT, page 83
to learn more about thumbnails.**

Tracking

Tracking is when you adjust the overall space between letters in a text selection. (It is also referred to as *letterspacing* in some programs.)

Use tracking to improve the overall appearance and readability of your type.

Tracking can also be a stylistic choice — there are times when you want your copy to have a tightly spaced look, while other times you may want a loose, airy look.

You can use tracking to fit more characters per line in case you have limited space and need to squeeze in an extra word or two.

Tracking adjusts space in very small increments. Different programs use different units to measure tracking — usually some fraction of an *em space*. An em space is the width of the letter "M" in your font. Some programs apply tracking in units of a point. When you adjust the space between a pair of letters only, this is called *kerning* (see KERNING, page 80).

Tracking is expressed as a negative or positive number, with zero reflecting no tracking adjustments at all.

DEMONSTRATION

This is a block of text with different tracking settings.

> We are proud that you have selected a pair of Alamo Boots. The Alamo Boot Company is known around the world for its fine quality leather footwear. Each pair of Alamo boots is hand-crafted from full-grain, cowhide leather. Superior craftsmanship and rugged good looks are what make Alamo boots superior.

This is 9 pt. Century Book, 0 tracking.

We are proud that you have selected a pair of
Alamo Boots. The Alamo Boot Company is
known around the world for its fine quality
leather footwear. Each pair of Alamo boots is
hand-crafted from full-grain, cowhide leather.
Superior craftsmanship and rugged good looks
are what make Alamo boots superior.

This is 9 pt. Century Book, +10 tracking (1/20 of an em space).

We are proud that you have selected a pair of Alamo
Boots. The Alamo Boot Company is known around the
world for its fine quality leather footwear. Each pair of
Alamo boots is hand-crafted from full-grain, cowhide
leather. Superior craftsmanship and rugged good looks are
what make Alamo boots superior.

This is 9 pt. Century Book, -10 tracking (-1/20 of an em space).

DESIGN TIPS

- For a stylish effect, add extra tracking to a short line
  of text. This works well on projects such as brochure
  covers, ads, and posters, where a single page needs to
  be particularly eye-catching. All capital letters work
  particularly well with this effect.

T H I N K   A B O U T   F L O R I D A   T H I S   Y E A R .

A N N U A L   R E P O R T

PRINCE   VLADIMIR   CHOCOLATES

**See KERNING, page 80,
to learn more about tracking.**

Trapping

Trapping is a printing term that refers to the slight overlap of colors that appear next to each other in a printed piece of artwork.

This is an advanced term concerning preparation for printing. It is primarily of interest if you are making film separations from your document. It is worth knowing if you use advanced page layout program features, or if you plan to become involved in printing. In trapping, one color "traps" the other by overlapping it slightly. This is done so that if any shift occurs on the printing press, there will not be a white space between objects.

DEMONSTRATION

In the example below, the light background represents a color (a different color than the letter A). This color would need to slightly overlap or *trap* the "A." The overlap is indicated below by the gray outline around the letter.

COMPUTER TIPS

- Most professional page layout programs have built-in trapping features or a related application that lets the user deal with trapping. We recommend that whenever possible, you let a professional deal with trapping — your printer or an expert at your service bureau (see SERVICE BUREAU, page 145).

Typeface abc

A typeface is a set of characters distinguished by specific style and design characteristics.

Every typeface has its own unique appearance. That appearance is determined by many factors, some of which include:

- **Serifs –** Shape and length.
- **Stroke – thickness** Variations in the letterform.
- **Roundness of letter forms** – Shape of the letter "o," for example.
- **X-height –** How large the lowercase letters are relative to the capital letters (see X-HEIGHT, page 184).
- **Shape of counters** – The size of letters with enclosed shapes like "o" and "a."
- **Length of ascenders and descenders** – Refers to the height of letters like "l" "h" and "k," and the depth of letters like "p" and "q."

These are only a few of the features that give a typeface its own identity. Look closely at any two typefaces and you'll see many ways in which each letter is unique.

There are hundreds of different typefaces. Some, like Helvetica and Times Roman, are more commonly used than others. Some typefaces come into style and appear everywhere for a few years and then drop out of sight, while others, like Caslon, remain in use for centuries.

Like people, every typeface has its own character. Some are casual and friendly in appearance, while others are austere and serious. That character is an essential part of why you choose one typeface over another.

Even the names of individual typefaces reflect their individual character and history. Typefaces are frequently named after the person who designed them. Frederic

Continued

TYPEFACE

Goudy, John Baskerville, Claude Garamond, Eric Gill, Ed Benguiat, and Herman Zapf all gave their names to type-faces. Others are named after a place: Memphis, Helvetica (Switzerland) and New York, for example. Finally, others — mainly display fonts — are named after the image they suggest, such as Rubber Stamp, Brush Script or Frankfurter.

The fact that there are hundreds of typefaces to choose from is daunting to many new designers. It is only with time and use that you become familiar with the multitude of typefaces. Many professional designers only use a limited selection of typefaces in their work, prefer-ring to work with ten or fifteen basic typefaces. It is not necessary to use all the typefaces, only the ones appro-priate for your work.

DEMONSTRATION

Take a close look at a three common letters. Notice how the letters vary from typeface to typeface. The tail of the letter "r" has a different shape in every typeface.

rug Gill Sans   rug Helvetica

rug Century   rug Times

rug Palatino   **rug** Miami Nights

rug Avant Garde   rug Bookman

Here are examples of common typefaces:

Bodoni	Korinna
Clearface	Memphis
Freestyle Script	**Optima**
Futura	Palatino
Garamond	Serif Gothic
Gill Sans	Stone Sans
Goudy	**Times**
Helvetica	Univers
Italia	*Zapf Chancery*

DESIGN TIPS

- When you choose a typeface, pick one that is appropriate for your project.

   This type is a little too bold and angular for a ballet program but it would work for a sports event or perhaps for an upbeat newsletter.

   This is 11 pt. Serifa Bold.

Continued

TYPEFACE

This is not an appropriate typeface for a software manual because it is old-fashioned. It is fine for an invitation or announcement.

This is 13 pt. Zapf Chancery.

This typeface may be too serious and impersonal for the logo of a business promoting a personal service (like a caterer or a day care center). But its aggressive, bold strokes make it ideal for a corporate document like a quarterly report.

This is 10.5 pt. Franklin Gothic Demi.

- Always make sure that your typeface is legible at the size you plan to use it.

- On the other hand, there are no rules — only guidelines. It's okay to break the rules, but only after you have gotten to know them well.

- If you happen to be working with a very large selection of typefaces and are having trouble choosing one , make a list of three or four possibilities. Then set a few lines of type from your actual project in each of the selected typefaces, and print the page. Once you see an example of how your job looks in each typeface, your choice will become easier.

- If you are designing a logo and are considering a few different typefaces, check out the particular letters of the alphabet that will be appearing in your logo. See how they work in combination. You may discover that while you like a certain typeface in general, the individual letters just don't work. For example, the letters in

174

this logo — "R," "L" and "K" — are the basis for this logo. Notice how different they are in each of the examples.

RLK
Rilroth LaTrege & Klieg
Investment Partners

RLK
Rilroth LaTrege & Klieg
Investment Partners

RLK
Rilroth LaTrege & Klieg
Investment Partners

RLK
Rilroth LaTrege & Klieg
Investment Partners

COMPUTER TIPS

• Different type and equipment manufacturers use different names for the same typeface. Helvetica, probably the most common typeface, goes by many names, such as: Helios, Swiss, Vega, Megaron, or Claro.

Note that when you purchase typefaces, not all of them are equally well designed and there may be slight differences between typefaces of the same name. Beware of typefaces that are inferior in design.

See **DISPLAY TYPE, page 41, FONT, page 51, TYPESTYLE, page 147;**
to learn more about typeface.

Type Family

A type family includes all the various weights and styles of a given typeface.

DEMONSTRATION

Below is an example of the Franklin Gothic family of type.

This is Franklin Gothic Book.

This is Franklin Gothic Book Oblique.

This is Franklin Gothic Demi.

This is Franklin Gothic Demi Oblique.

This is Franklin Gothic Heavy.

This is Franklin Gothic Heavy Oblique.

This is Franklin Gothic Regular Condensed.

This is Franklin Gothic Extra Condensed.

Typestyle a **b** *c*

Typestyle refers to variations in the style of a single typeface. Typestyle variations change the appearance of a typeface, without changing the features that make it recognizable.

In traditional typography, typestyle includes variations in a typeface's weight and width, as well as effects such as outlining and drop shadows. Other typestyles include italic, small caps, extended or condensed type, superior or inferior characters and others.

Many typestyle variations are available as menu selections in many programs (where they are often called, simply, *styles*. Some of the choices you will find on typestyle menus are:

- Plain
- *Italic*
- Shadow
- Word Underline
- SMALL CAPS
- Super^{script}
- Superior

- **Bold**
- Outline
- Underline
- ~~Strike Through~~
- ALL CAPS
- Sub_{script}
- Inferior

NOTE: Superior and inferior type are used for footnotes, mathematical expressions and scientific notation. You can also use them to create fractions.

Again, all of these options change some aspect of the type's appearance without changing the typeface's basic character.

Continued

DEMONSTRATION

All of these are considered variations in typestyle:

Century Light
Century Book
Century Bold
Century Ultra

Century Book Italic
Century Italic Bold
Century Ultra Italic

Century Condensed
Century Expanded

Century Bold Outline

CENTURY BOOK SMALL CAPS

Century Bold Shadow

Century Book Underline

~~Century Book Strike through~~

CENTURY BOOK CAPS

DESIGN TIPS

- Typestyle is often used to add emphasis. For example:

    Whatever you do, *don't panic*.

    Now, we're making this **free offer** available to you.

    Ours is the *only* healthcare plan to offer
    full coverage.

    This is offer is for a limited time only. DON'T WAIT!

- If you use typestyle to create emphasis, it is most effective in moderation. Don't emphasize everything or it will make your use of different typestyles meaningless:

    Don't emphasize *everything* or it will make your use of *different* typestyles MEANINGLESS. *Too many typestyles in **one block of text** will give your readers A HEADACHE.*

- There is an exception to every rule, including this one. It's okay to mix lots of typestyles if you want to create the novelty look of an old-fashioned poster. For example:

JOIN

THE ALAMO BOOT COMPANY
For their SPRING ROUND-UP
of NEW FASHIONS

AT

Special Reduced Prices
DON'T MISS IT!

Uppercase

Uppercase letters are capital letters.

   Uppercase and lowercase are traditional printer terms for capital and small letters. The terms refer to the actual wooden cases that were once used to store type (when it was set by hand).

DEMONSTRATION

These are uppercase letters:

ABCDEFGHIJKLMNOP QRSTUVWXYZ

DESIGN TIPS

• If you are writing instructions that specify a line of type should be upper- and lowercase, the correct abbreviation is U&lc or U/lc.

**See CAPITAL LETTERS, page 19
SMALL CAPS, page 159**
to learn more about upper- and lowercase letters.

White Space

White space refers to the parts of your page where no type or graphics appear.

Although white space is nothing more than the empty areas of the page, graphic designers consider white space an important part of their design. That's because copy needs space to "breathe," in order to be comfortably enjoyed by the reader. Remember, no matter how interesting your copy is, it won't be eye-catching or noticeable in the middle of clutter.

White space might include your margins, the area around a picture, the space between headings, the space between logos and text, or the space between words.

DEMONSTRATION

This is an example of an ad that makes extensive use of white space in its design.

$\mathscr{P}$rince Vladimir chocolates;
Simply the finest sweets
the world has ever known.

Prince
Vladimir
fine chocolates since 1750

Continued

DESIGN TIPS

- For an especially elegant and understated look, try positioning a small block of copy — tastefully — on a page with a lot of white space. As in the previous ad, copy does not have to be large to be noticeable:

❧

*The Edison Grande is planning
Thanksgiving Dinner this year.
Imagine: delicious food, no dishes, and
a view of the Hudson. Sound good?*

❧

*Call for reservations.
(212)555-7000
The Edison Grand Hotel
Grand Falls, New York*

**See GRAPHIC DESIGN, page 60
to learn more about white space.**

Widows

A widow is a word that sits alone on a line at the end of a paragraph or at the top of a page.

Graphic designers consider widows poor design because a word alone on a line — particularly a short one — is distracting.

DEMONSTRATION

The last word in this sentence is considered a widow:

> Passengers were skeptical as they prepared to voyage across the English Channel in the new Eurotunnel. While many looked forward to the speed and efficiency of a trip across the Channel by shuttle, others said they would miss the experience of crossing the Channel on the deck of a ferry.

DESIGN TIPS

• If you format a block of copy and end up with a widow, you have several options. First you can edit the copy. Since that is not always an option, however, here are a few other steps you can take in order to reflow the copy. Your goal is to get words to shift up or down a line, in order to make the text break differently.

Change your line width.

Track the type tighter (see TRACKING page 168).

Insert a break in the copy yourself. This may help the copy to flow differently.

• Under no circumstances leave the end of a hyphenated word alone on a line.

X-height

The x-height of a font is the height of a lowercase letter without ascenders (h, l, k, t,) or descenders (g, p,q, y). It is the height of the letter "x."

X-height reflects the relationship between upper- and lowercase letters. If you look at two typefaces at exactly the same size, the typeface with the smaller x-height will *appear smaller* in size than the typeface with a larger x-height. X-height is a key factor in determining the overall appearance of a typeface.

X-height and leading tend to work together. If you are using a typeface with a very small x-height, your copy will appear to have more space between lines.

DEMONSTRATION

This is how x-height is measured:

These are four different typefaces, all set in 32 pt. As you can see, the size of the lowercase letters vary greatly from font to font.

Yes   Yes   Yes   Yes

Cochin   Palatino   Helvetica   Avant Garde

Here is is a block of copy set in four typefaces, to show how x-heights affects linespacing. All four paragraphs are set 9/11 (9 pt. type with 11 pt. leading).

In the new film, *Café Morocco*, Hughie Broderick plays detective Sam Gum, sent to explore the strange disappearance of a restaurant owner. As Gum probes the back rooms of the Café Morroco, he finds that nothing is what it seems to be.

In the new film, *Café Morocco*, Hughie Broderick plays detective Sam Gum, sent to explore the strange disappearance of a restaurant owner. As Gum probes the back rooms of the Café Morroco, he finds that nothing is what it seems to be.

In the new film, *Café Morocco*, Hughie Broderick plays detective Sam Gum, sent to explore the strange disappearance of a restaurant owner. As Gum probes the back rooms of the Café Morroco, he finds that nothing is what it seems to be.

In the new film, *Café Morocco*, Hughie Broderick plays detective Sam Gum, sent to explore the strange disappearance of a restaurant owner. As Gum probes the back rooms of the Café Morroco, he finds that nothing is what it seems to be.

DESIGN TIPS

• If you are trying to fit copy into a small space, try using a typeface with a small x-height. More characters will fit on a line than if you select a larger typeface, and you can use a smaller leading setting.

Part II:

Design Templates

On the following pages, you will find samples of logos, ads, newsletters, stationery and more, with instructions on how you can make similar artwork using your own copy. Choose the style that best suits your needs, and then apply the instructions that come with each sample.

The artwork you will see includes simple pieces that you can create with any word processing program, as well as complex art that advanced desktop publishers can create using more sophisticated layout and type programs. The samples are labeled *Easy, Intermediate,* and *Advanced* using symbols (see below).

There are some design samples you will not be able to produce with your particular program; don't get frustrated. Whether you are a beginner or an expert, this design template section is meant to provide you with ideas and possibilities. Use them as a basis for your own artwork, and adjust them to your needs and skill level.

Let the following design ideas be a beginning for your own creative exploration of desktop publishing and graphic design.

1. Logos, type only

Henry HAWTHORNE
C O L L E G E

Goudy

■ THREE WORD LOGO
Set the first word in **upper and lowercase** letters and the second word **all caps**. Put a black bar underneath the second word. **Reverse** the business title (ie. Company, College) from the black bar. **Kern** letters to width of bar.

Henry ❧ Hawthorne
C O L L E G E

Clearface

■ THREE WORD LOGO
Set name in **upper and lowercase** letters, flush left. Take the business title and set it smaller, **letterspacing** it to the length of the word above it. If the first word is short, add a **dingbat** next to it, as we did here.

HENRY HAWTHORNE
COLLEGE

Copperplate and Janson

■ THREE WORD LOGO
The center word is the focus of this logo. Set it in all caps and larger letters than the other two words — approximately twice as big. Make the first word **flush left** and the third word **flush right**. Try using two different typefaces.

CURTIS
construction co.

Gill Sans

● TWO OR THREE WORD LOGO
Set the main title in an **italic** typeface, **all caps**. Set the second word in the same typeface, also italic. Make second word all **lowercase**, and position it hanging to the right of the logo.

1. Logos, type only

CURTIS
CONSTRUCTION CO.

Futura

● TWO OR THREE
WORD LOGO
Set the first word in **bold
caps**. Set the words
underneath to fit the
width of the first word.
Set these in the **regular**
weight of same typeface.

**Curtis
Construction
Company**

Clearface

● TWO OR THREE
WORD LOGO
Set words on different
lines, **flush left**. Add a
drop shadow to the
typeface. Put a **border**
around the words with a
thickness of two or three
points.

AUSTIN
S W I M   C L U B

Franklin Gothic and Kabel

■ TWO OR THREE
WORD LOGO
Set the first word in **all
caps**. Add a **drop
shadow**. Kern the letters
out a little so name has
an airy look. In small
type, set the other words
to justify with the name
above. **Letterspace** the
word to fit. Try using two
different typefaces.

Austin
swim club

Bodoni

■ TWO OR THREE
WORD LOGO
Set the first words in
caps/lowercase. Set the
other word(s) smaller, in
regular italic. Position
at right of first word, as
shown.

Austin
S W I M   C L U B

Futura

In the second exam-
ple, we did the same
thing, only we used a
sans serif typeface, and
we set the smaller words
in **all caps**.

1. Logos, type only

Gill Sans and Janson

● THREE WORD LOGO
This logo lends itself to use with a personal name. Set the first word in **italic caps and lowercase**. Set the second name **all caps**, with no space between the two names. Set the company name underneath, in **italics**. **Track** to width of name.

ANN ELK *interiors*

Helvetica and Bodoni

● TWO OR THREE WORD LOGO
Set the company name in **bold all caps**. Set the company name or business title next to it in **lowercase italics**. Underline all with a 3 pt. rule.

Snell Roundhand and Avant Garde

■ TWO OR THREE WORD LOGO
Set the first word in **a script**. Put the company name or business title underneath in a **sans serif** typeface, **reversed** from a small horizontal box (or bar). Center the bar.

GONZALES
EMPLOYMENT SERVICES

Helvetica Condensed

■ TWO OR THREE WORD LOGO
Set the first words in **all italic caps**. Use a **sans serif** typeface. Set the business title **all caps**. **Letterspace slightly**. The second typeface should not be italic. Underline with a half-point rule (.5pt). Check that the first and second line align in an attractive way!

● = EASY   ■ = INTERMEDIATE   ▲ = ADVANCED   **189**

II. Logos with initials

RLK

Rilroth, Latrege & Klieg
Investment Partners

Bodoni and Avant Garde

● INITIALS
Set the first word in a
serif typeface, and the full
business title underneath
(indented slightly here) in
much smaller **caps and
lowercase** letters, **flush
left**.

RLK

Rilroth, Latrege & Klieg
Investment Partners

Avant Garde and Bodoni

● INITIALS
Here we reversed the
type choices above. The
large initials are set in
sans serif and the business title is in a **serif** typeface. Lines are centered.

RLK

Rilroth, La Trege & Klieg
Investment Partners

Cochin and Helvetica

■ INITIALS
Set the initials in a **serif**
typeface. The business
name is **flush left** on two
lines, positioned to **align**
with the top of the large
initials. The full business
name is set in **italic sans
serif** type.

RLK

Rilroth
Latrege
& Klieg

Investment Partners

Cochin and Helvetica

■ INITIALS
Set the initials in a **serif**
typeface. Put the compa-
ny's full name on three
lines (or two if you are
using only two initial letters) so that they are
flush with the height and
baseline of the initials.
Here we put the business
title underneath the name
in **caps** and **lowercase**.

RLK

Rilroth, Latrege & Klieg
Investment Partners

Futura

● INITIALS
Take the boldest sans serif
type you can find. Use for
initials. Set full name
underneath in a corre-
sponding light typeface.

II. Logos with initials

INVESTMENT PARTNERS

Helvetica and Helvetica Compressed

■ INITIALS
Create a vertical box with a **blend** that goes from dark to light at the bottom. In front of this, place your initials in white, centered in the box and **aligned** with the bottom of the box. Underneath the box, **flush left**, place the full name and/or business title. Here we used a smaller typeface set in **sans serif, italic all caps**. Try this same layout with a solid black box.

RILROTH, LATREGE & KLIEG
INVESTMENT PARTNERS

Futura and Helvetica

▲ INITIALS
Set initials in **extra bold, all caps italic**. On top of the initials, position white rules of thickness that goes from very thin (half pt.) to heavy (3 pt.). There are many ways to do this, depending on the program you are working in. Under the initials, set the full company name. Here we used a **medium** and a **lighter** typeface.

Sanchez and Needleman
Attorneys at Law

Bookman

▲ INITIALS
Set the initials in a **serif** typeface. Add a **drop shadow**. Position a thick rule on both the top and the bottom initials, (equal distance from the letters). The rules used in the example are 8 pt. Underneath the bottom rule, set the full company name in the same typeface you used for the initials. Center it, and if necessary, condense width.

III. Logos with graphics

In order to create these logos, you will need some sort of artwork that you can import into your program. You can use clip art, scans, metafiles, or graphics you create yourself in a drawing program.

■ SIMPLE GRAPHICS
At right are logos that were all created by setting the company name in a typeface that suited the nature of the business, and then adding a simple graphic.

A graphic can be centered over the name, flush left or flush right, or positioned underneath the title. In some cases, we let the name run around the graphic.

Note that the graphic supports the company name, without overpowering it.

The typefaces used in the logos at left are, from top logo to bottom:
Serifa
Bodoni
Cochin and Kauffman
Futura
Helvetica

III. Logos with graphics

Bodoni

■ THREE WORD LOGO
Set your copy in **reverse** in a **black box**. Put your picture to the right of the box, and **scale** it so that it is slightly *smaller* than the height of your box. Put a **frame** or **border** around the picture. Make it the same height as the box with the copy.

Goudy

▲ TWO OR THREE WORD LOGO
Put your graphic in a box. You will need a picture against a dark background to make this work. Set the type directly beneath the box, **letterspacing** the words so they are just short of the full width of the box. You can make your copy all the same size, or make your copy different sizes as we did here. Put a **frame** around the graphics and type.

Gill Sans

● TWO OR THREE WORD LOGO
Next to your graphic, on the left, place your company or organization name. Set in **caps and lowercase.** Beneath this, lining up with the right of the graphic, set the business title. In this case, "literacy volunteers" is one third the size of the words, "Helping Hand."

III. Logos with graphics

The logos below were all created using advanced graphics techniques. If you use a drawing program, you can create some of the effects below yourself, for example, curved type, and special shaped graphics.

▲ CURVED TYPE
Set your company name so that it **curves** around a graphic placed in the center. Underneath the graphic, **reverse** the business title in white from a black bar.

Kabel

Triplex and Futura

▲ GRAPHICS THAT REPLACE LETTERS
Let a graphic (usually, but not always specially designed) replace one of the letters in your logo. In the "Wildcat Video Productions" logo, the cat replaces the letter "A". In "John's Tropical Fish" the fish graphic replaces the letter "O."

Bodoni and Kauffman

III. Logos with graphics

Try creating custom graphics (graphics specially designed for a particular logo, as opposed to generic clip art). Even a simple graphic can work, as shown in the Mr. Lawn logos below.

MR. LAWN
L A N D S C A P I N G

Futura

*Franklin Gothic
and Bodoni
(below)*

■ CUSTOM GRAPHICS
Set the product or service name in **bold uppercase** letters. Set the business title in **uppercase** letters, about one third the size of the type in the first line. **Track** type to the width of the first line. Place your graphic above the name.

In the other two Mr. Lawn logos, we used a simple graphic of grass. In the first example, all the type — including punctuation — is **justified**. In the second example, the title is set in **caps and lowercase extra bold** type. The type of business, landscaping, is set in *italic* type about half the size of the first line, **flush right**.

**MR.
LAWN**
LANDSCAPING

Mr. Lawn
Landscaping

WILDCAT
VIDEO PRODUCTIONS

▲ CUSTOM GRAPHICS
Create a custom graphic that has a square format. Place your company name beneath the graphic, **centered.** Select a size so that your name runs the full length of the graphic. In this case, we let it run slightly wider than the graphic.

Futura

IV. Logos with tints (shades)

A tint or a shade is a very effective way to add "color" to a logo. Below are various ways to use shades and tints to enliven a logo.

Hopewell Medical Center

Helvetica

● TINTED TYPE
Apply a different **shade** to each line (or word) in your logo. In this case, the first word has a 70% shade, the second word a 50% shade, and the third word a 30% shade. We tightened the **leading** in this logo so that the lines of type overlap.

HOT TAMALES
Mexican Food

Franklin Gothic and Kauffman

● TINTED TYPE
Apply a different **shade** to two words next to each other. This has a very eye-catching effect. The first word has a shade of 70%. The second word has a shade of 40%.

JACK CATS
PET SUPPLY

Goudy and Futura

● TINTED TYPE
In this example, the first word has a shade of 35% and the second word, 65%

Bodoni and Franklin Gothic Condensed

■ TINTED TYPE
Set your logo on several lines. In this case, we made the main name in the title (Elk) about three times larger than the other words. Set the central name in solid black. Apply a **shade** to the other words. Here we **reversed** the business title out of a bar with a tint. Be careful that type doesn't break up and become illegible when you reverse it from a bar, and don't make the tint too light.

IV. Logos with tints (shades)

Goudy

TYPE OVERLAYING TINTED CHARACTERS
Set your company initials, a dingbat, or other character in a large size, with a **shade** of 20%. On top of this, position your company name in **solid black** type. Note that not all programs let you create this effect.

café**BERNICE**

Bodoni and Bodoni Poster

TYPE OVERLAYING TINTED CHARACTERS
This logo suits a shorter name. Set the name with a **shade** — here we used 30%. Set the related business title in **solid black**. Position so that it overlaps the name.

PHOTOplaza

Futura

TYPE OVERLAYING TINTED CHARACTERS
This logo demonstrates the same effect as the example above. Here we added a **rule.** Both have a shade of 50%.

Bellevue and Caslon

▲ **TYPE OVERLAYING A TINTED BOX**
Set your company name in a box filled with a light **shade** (20% or 30%). Set the type in black and position it **flush right**. Leave space to left of type. In this space, set a symbol or character. Make it white. This effect requires some juggling with size in order to make everything fit nicely. Again, you will only be able to create this logo with a program that allows precise type manipulation.

V. Logos, fun

The logos below show you some of the more advanced ways of handling type and graphics. Many of the special type effects were created in a drawing program (Adobe Illustrator). We include them here to give you an idea of your creative options in logo design.

V. Logos, fun

VI. Stationery layouts

The next pages will show you sample stationery set layouts. Each page includes a letterhead (the 8 1/2" x 11" piece of writing paper), a #10 envelope (a standard business envelope) and a business card. All are reduced to fit on the page.

Below the layout is an actual-size business card so you can better see the use of type.

In designing stationery, your goal is to make all pieces coordinate. The letterhead, business card, and envelope, as well as labels, should look like they belong together. The typestyle you use should remain the same from piece to piece. Your layout will have to change slightly due to the different shapes of the different items, however.

VI. Stationery layouts

CURTIS
construction co.

114 Central Business Park North • Plankston, NJ 23950 • Tel: (908) 555-1970 • Fax: (908) 555-1975

CURTIS
construction co.

Fred Rowlands
President

114 Central Business Park North • Plankston, NJ 23950
Tel: (908) 555-1970 • Fax: (908) 555-1975

CURTIS
construction co.

114 Central Business Park North • Plankston, NJ 23950

CURTIS
construction co.

Fred Rowlands
President

114 Central Business Park North • Plankston, NJ 23950
Tel: (908) 555-1970 • Fax: (908) 555-1975

201

VI. Stationery layouts

VI. Stationery layouts

203 Troubador Pass • Mt. Guenevere, WA 23057 • (205)555-0958

203 Troubador Pass
Mt. Guenevere, WA 23057
Telephone (206) 555-0958

203 Troubador Pass
Mt. Guenevere, WA 23057

203 Troubador Pass
Mt. Guenevere, WA 23057
Telephone (206) 555-0958

A business card does not always have to be horizontal; here is an example of a vertical layout.

VI. Stationery layouts

1515 Lantern Bay Drive, St. Petersburg FL 06123 (407)555-9900

VI. Stationery layouts

Sanchez & Needleman Attorneys

Sanchez & Needleman Attorneys

Esther Needleman
Senior Partner

1957 Amond Ave. Suite 14
Trufflestone, CT 01572
Tel (203) 555-9746
Fax (203) 555-9740

Sanchez & Needleman Attorneys

1957 Amond Ave. Suite 14
Trufflestone, CT 01572

Sanchez & Needleman Attorneys

Esther Needleman
Senior Partner

1957 Amond Ave. Suite 14
Trufflestone, CT 01572
Tel (203) 555-9746
Fax (203) 555-9740

VII. Ad Designs

The challenge of designing ads is to fit text, graphics, and logos into a fixed space, while keeping all your material readable. The way to do this is by prioritizing your information. Determine what your most important message is, and let this information stand out. Keep your message clear and simple, and make sure your ad is easy to read at a glance.

Below are some examples of small ads.

In the ad above, the most prominent information is the logo. The second most important feature is "Poetry Reading." We added a panel at the far right with a graphic reversed from a shaded box.

We designed this ad to look like a coupon. The main point here is the "Save $10" offer. We echoed this headline by repeating "$10" in the four corners.

VII. Ad Designs

Come to
Café Bernice on
Wednesdays for our
all-you-can-eat
pasta dinner special!

Only
$12.95
per person.

café **BERNICE**

NORTHERN ITALIAN CUISINE

214 East Michigan Avenue
(corner of Williams)
West Tyler (202) 555-1230
open seven days

Pasta That's Perfection

This ad is divided into two parts. On the left is a boxed special that is clearly set apart from the rest of the information. On the right is all the basic information about the restaurant with the logo being the most prominent feature and the tag line, "Pasta That's Perfection" being the second prominent feature.

Nov. 17-21

Join us for the 18th Annual
Morristown
Country Fair!

At the Morristown
Community
Center
418 Post Road
10am — 4pm
FREE ADMISSION

Featuring:
• Craft Demonstrations from Local Crafts People
• Food & Games
• Live performances
• Handmade goods for sale

In this ad we used a graphic in the lower right. It's balanced on the upper right by a burst containing the dates of the event. We used a clip art border to make the ad more eye-catching. The title of the event stands out in this ad.

VII. Ad Designs

Spring Bonanza!

All misses and junior dresses now 30-50% off!

Save on all jewelry and accessories too! Every department is filled with major markdowns. Hurry in for the best selection!

All your favorite designers for less!

47 Rte. 11-A • Tremont Mall • Mon.–Sat., 9am –8pm. Credit cards accepted

The main focus of this ad is the heading, "Spring Bonanza!" Notice that we combined italic initial caps with regular roman text. Because this is a Spring fashion ad, we kept the ad airy and light. On the left, set in script, is the tag line "All your favorite designers for less!" which is large, but not so large that it competes with the heading.

GOULD, ROGERS & KANE

TAX PREPARATION

This tax season, let our experts prepare your taxes and financial statements. We have over 35 years of experience in the field of tax preparation. Call us today at:

(303)555-8100

Gould, Rogers & Kane
Gladeston Mall
West of I-95

Don't gamble with your finances!

This is a simple ad whose main point is the service provided — tax preparation. The second most important information is the company's phone number. We put a graphic in the lower right to make the otherwise all-text ad a little more lively. Also note we put a drop shadow on the heading.

VII. Ad Designs

Below are larger display ads. In these ads we have more space than in the previous ads which in turn lets us use larger graphics. Also, notice that there is more of an emphasis on copywriting in the following ads.

You don't have to own one of these to get the most out of your garden.

Our trained staff can help you grow vegetables like the professionals.

12 Main Rd (next to the library). Open 7 Days • Mon. - Fri. 9-11 • Sat.-Sun.
Call the Elroy Service Line for location information and gardening advice at (718) VEGGIES.

The headline is the main focus of this ad. The heading and the graphic are both centered, as are the logo and the address.

VII. Ad Designs

It used to be that you had to
head west to get quality boots...

...not anymore.

over 100 locations nationwide

or call 1-800-555-Boots to find
a distributor near you.

This ad also uses a centered (clip art) graphic as the focus of attention. The
headline is set above the picture and note that it continues below the picture in
the same typeface and size. We added a rough, rope-like border to make the ad
more rugged looking, keeping with the Western theme.

VII. Ad Designs

In this add we applied a tint of 30% to the graphic, and put it in the background, behind the headline.

VII. Ad Designs

Autumn

The perfect time for a weekend getaway. The weather and scenery of the New England countryside have never been more beautiful. Come visit us at the Laughing Moon Inn and experience the magic of the season.

Full bed and breakfast

203 Troubador Pas, Mt. Guenivere, VT 23057   (343) 257-0958

The ad above makes ample use of white space. The border has a 50% shade applied to it.

VII. Ad Designs

This ad uses a headline in reverse and a thick border. The logo runs the full width of the ad.

VII. Ad Designs

In the ad above, we wrapped the type around a large graphic (this is called a runaround). Notice that the graphic goes right to the border.

We applied a shade to the graphic of 25% so it prints lightly. The logo appears in the lower right.

VII. Ad Designs

Since the ad above is for the same company (the Austin Swim Club), we placed the logo in exactly the same position as in the previous ad. This gives the advertisements consistency. This ad takes a very visual approach to conveying its message, and uses pictures instead of words to make its point.

VII. Ad Designs

HAVEN'T HAD MUCH TIME TO DO THE YARD WORK LATELY?

Call Jim McGee's Yard Cleaning Service

(415) 555-2395 • Page: (917) 555-1243

Cut out this ad and bring it in for a 20% discount!

● *Serving the community for 12 years.* ●

This is a simple ad, based on a headline that is centered in the middle of a graphic. Copy is organized beneath it with the name of the company being most prominent. The border is dashed, suggesting that the reader cut the ad out.

VII. Ad Designs

"It's too rich..."

"I just can't..."

"I'm on a diet.

"I really have to watch what I eat..."

"I know that I won't be able to eat just one..."

"I shouldn't"

"I'll spoil my dinner..."

INDULGE YOURSELF

(we won't tell anyone)

prince vladimir chocolates

This ad employs the graphic design technique of using many different shades (or tints) within one design.

VIII. Newsletter Designs

These newsletter samples illustrate different options in laying out a publication. The newsletter below uses a three column format or grid. The text appears in the two columns on the right. The first column contains the organization's logo and the table of contents.

Use symbol or logo here.

Full name of organization is set above the publication title. Note the drop shadow on "NEWS."

HHC

HENRY HAWTHORNE COLLEGE ALUMNI

NEWS

Summer Edition   Vol. II, No. 4

Class of '68 returns for Spring Parade and Reunion picnic

Over 200 people marched, skipped, and hopped past the Statue of Knowledge last month as part of the annual reunion of the Class of '68. Several decades have passed since members of the class

Spring parade marches on as Class of '68 reunites.

of '68 spent days and nights in The Weintraub Library, before slipping over to Milt's Hamburger Hut for late night burgers and Milt's famous malt. Milt's has been replaced with an eight story dormitory but it seems the class of '68 can still carry a tune — several of our former band members donned their band uniforms and hefted their instruments for a rendition of the Henry Hawthorne fight song. Members of the pep squad built a float and joined the Spring Parade. Alum Daniel Berns supplied the horses. Sandra Coates, Ginny Perkins, Mark Baldwin and Fred Gould led the crowd in

an old cheer before announcing reunion awards.

This year's reunion awards went to a number of deserving classmates. The most prestigious award went to Carla Wong Desoto who was recognized with the Hawthorne Humanitarian award for her contribution to education. As teacher and principle in the public school system, Carla has change the lives of countless students who have benefited from her teaching and moral support. The prize for Most Successful Classmate went to Matt Greenberg, who has made a name for himself as America's industrial parts king.

con't on page 5

CONTENTS

Table of contents is in bold to set it apart from the rest of the text.

Note hanging initial cap at start of story. We used the same typeface as we used in the publication title (Helvetica).

VIII. Newsletter Designs

This newsletter uses a two column format and allows pictures (as well as the table of contents) to extend beyond the edge of the column into the margins.

Name of publication
is in bold serif type.

In this example, the logo of the organization is centered beneath the title publication. We used a bar with a tint to separate the name of the publication from the text.

The cap calls tion the t of ory.

Henry Hawthrone Collge Alumni

NEWS

Summer Edition

HHC

Class of '68 Returns

Over 200 people marched, skipped, and hopped past the Statue of Knowledge last month as part of the annual reunion of the Class of '68. Several decades have passed since members of the class of '68 spent days and nights in The Weintraub Library, before slipping over to Milt's Hamburger Hut for late night burgers and Milt's famous malt. Milt's has been replaced with an eight story dormitory but it seems the class of '68 can still carry a tune — several of our former band members donned their band uniforms and hefted their instruments

for a rendition of the Henry Hawthorne fight song. Members of the pep squad built a float and joined the Spring Parade. Alum Daniel Berns supplied the horses. Sandra Coates, Ginny Perkins, Mark Baldwin and Fred Gould led the crowd in an old cheer before announcing reunion awards.

CONTENTS

This year's reunion awards went to a number of deserving classmates. The most prestigious award went to Carla Wong Desoto who was recognized with the Hawthorne Humanitarian award for her contribution to education. As teacher and principle in the public school system, Carla has change the lives of countless students who have benefited from her teaching and moral support. The prize for Most Successful Classmate went to Matt Greenberg, who has made a name for himself as America's industrial parts king. And the award for Continuing Contribution to Henry Hawthorne College went con't on page 5

Spring parade marches on as Class of '68 reunites.

Photo runs beyond the column into the margin. It bleeds (runs to edge of page).

Contents is reversed from a black box in this newsletter. Note that like the photo, it runs beyond the edge of the column, into the margin.

VIII. Newsletter Designs

This newsletter uses a three column format. The name of the organization is set to the right of the publication title. The title is reversed from a black box.

Your box can be as wide as necessary to fit your publication title.

In this example, headlines are set in sans serif type.

 **HENRY HAWTHORNE COLLEGE**

HHC

Summer Edition

Vol. II, No. 4

Class of '68 returns for reunion

Over 200 people marched, skipped, and hopped past the Statue of Knowledge last month as part of the annual reunion of the Class of '68. Several decades have passed since members of the class of '68 spent days and nights in The Weintraub Library, before slipping over to Milt's Hamburger Hut for late night burgers and Milt's famous malt. Milt's has been replaced with an eight story dormitory but it seems the class of '68 can still carry a tune — several of our former band members donned their band uniforms and hefted their instruments for a rendition of the Henry Hawthorne fight song. Members of the pep squad built a float and joined the Spring Parade. Alum Daniel Berns supplied the horses. Sandra Coates, Ginny Perkins, Mark Baldwin and Fred Gould led the

Spring parade marches on as Class of '68 celebrates.

crowd in an old cheer before announcing reunion awards.

This year's reunion awards went to a number of deserving classmates. The most prestigious award went to Carla Wong Desoto who was recognized with the Hawthorne Humanitarian award for her contribution to education. As teacher and principle in the public school system, Carla has change the lives of countless students who

have benefited from her teaching and moral support. The prize for Most Successful Classmate went

CONTENTS

This layout uses rules between columns.

The table of contents is boxed with a drop shadow

IX. Leaflets

Leaflets or flyers are used to promote sales and events as well as goods and services. In the example below, the lower half of the page is used to promote sale items, while the top half of the page promotes the store itself. The heading, "Summer Sale!" separates the two halves. This leaflet uses a silhouetted photograph (halftone) as well as other types of graphics.

At Albright's All-Natural Isn't a Trend.

These days, with so much discussion about health and the environment, buying all-natural food is considered trendy is some circles. It isn't just a trend at Albright's. We've been selling all natural fruit and produce for over thirty years. And many of our customers have been with us since the beginning; now that's commitment.

At Albright's we believe in the value of good health. If you're looking for a place where all-natural is a way of life, come to Albright's, for the best in natural foods.

> **We carry only the highest quality foods and products.**

SUMMER SALE!

Just in! A variety of fresh summer fruits and vegetables, all on sale now.

Fresh Cherries
$1.^{49} *per lb.*

Black Plums
$1.^{25} *per lb.*

Bartlett Pears
$1.^{99} *per lb.*

Strawberries
$1.^{25} *per lb.*

Red Grapes
$2.^{49} *per lb.*

Peaches
$1.^{75} *per lb.*

To go anywhere else just isn't natural.
ALBRIGHT'S • *57* MAIN AVENUE • NEWTON EIGHTS

IX. Leaflets

This leaflet promotes an event — a New Year's Eve dinner. Note the way the main body text is divided into two parts. An illustration in the first part counterbalances an illustration in the second part. We used a fancy script for the headline, and set an initial cap in the same script. This leaflet uses various combinations of bold, italic, and small cap typestyles.

New Year's Eve
...at the Edison Grande Hotel

T his year, this Edison Grande Hotel will be ringing in the New Year in style. Award-winning Chef Michel has prepared a sumptuous, seven-course, prix-fixe dinner for this special occaision.

A fter dinner, dance the night away with the spectacular sounds of

ANNE HAMPTON CALLAWAY
AND HER ORCHESTRA

They will be playing all of your favorites, with that special flair that makes every performance a celebration.

Price is $45 per person.

Make your reservations early.

We will be happy to accept your reservations at

(316) 449-8200.

Finally—New Year's Eve done right!

IX. Leaflets

This leaflet promotes a sale. Notice the different sizes of copy used. The most prominent information is the name of the company. The body copy wraps around a picture of boots. A burst is used to call attention to credit card information. We put a border around the full page, and selected one that reflected the feeling of the leaflet itself (also used in the ad for the same company. See page 210).

We're having a round-up at the

Alamo Boot Company
Warehouse Outlet

We've got more boots than our barn can hold
— so it's time to move 'em out!

Come on down and rustle yourself up a pair of hand-crafted Alamo Boots. We sell only the finest shoes and boots, in hundreds of styles and colors. Check out the *Cowboy Hall of Fame* collection and give yourself the look of custom boots. Choose from stitched and appliquéd designs of hearts, flames, eagles, stars and more.

Hurry on in for the best selection—
at prices like these, there might
just be a stampede!

All Major Credit Cards Accepted

Alamo Boot Company Warehouse
Exit 242 East Jacksboro Highway
Telephone: 324-4243

Since this is a warehouse clearance, all
sales are final.

Glossary

Below are words that were not included in the definitions section of the book. Also included are alternate terms for many of the definitions.

A4 A standard size of the ISO (International Standards Organization) system used in Europe. This size is closest to the North American letter page of 8 ½" x 11".

Anchoring Postioning and attaching a frame or picture box to the text, so that it maintains the same relative position in the document despite reflowing.

Anti-aliasing A technique in photo-retouching programs for removing undesirable hard edges.

Ascender The upper part of a lowercase letter that rises above the x-height of a typeface, for example, l, k and h.

ASCII An acronym for American Standard Code for Information Interchange. A standard format for encoding data. (See FORMATS, page 47)

Author's alteration A correction or revision to a job requested by a client not based on errors made by the computer artist or operator.

Background The area of a photograph or illustration that is behind the main subject.

Bar code Another word for a U.P.C. code, the Universal Product Code that is printed on most packaging. A bar code is the pattern of varying vertical lines that contain pricing, product type and other information.

Basis weight The weight of a ream (500 sheets) of paper, cut to a standard size.

Continued

Bézier A type of curve that is defined mathematically by control points. Bézier curves are used by many drawing programs.

Binary A machine level code for encoding data.

Binding Various ways of attaching and securing sheets of paper in a book, journal, catalog or other publication. There are many types of binding including: saddle-stitch, perfect, ring-binding, GVC and others.

Blind embossing A relief impression made in paper without using any ink.

Blueprints Inexpensive proofs that printers make, as a last opportunity to review a job before printing.

Brochure A short publication promoting or describing a product, service or organization. A brochure is often a booklet with several pages bound together.

Burst The starlike shape that is used to grab attention. Bursts usually appear in ads or fliers and contain text (like the word "sale.").

Byline Credit line given to the author in a newspaper or magazine article.

Byte A unit composed of eight bits of information that is based on the binary system.

Calligraphy Stylized, decorative hand lettering. Calligraphy is usually used on fancy invitations and award certificates.

Camera-ready artwork Art that is ready to used in the printing process. Camera-ready means the artwork is ready to be photographed and converted into film.

Caption The short phrase that accompanies and explains a picture, photograph or cartoon.

CMYK Cyan, Magenta, Yellow and Black — the four basic colors of process printing (four color printing). (See COLOR OFFSET PRINTING, page 28.)

Color separation The preparation of art for printing by creating a different sheet of film for every color ink that will be used in a job.

Comp Short for *comprehensive artwork*. A comp is a finished dummy or mock-up of a job. A graphic designer produces comps in order to show a client different design options.

Contrast The range of difference between the darkest and the lightest tones in an image.

Cursive type Type that is similar to script, in that it resembles handwriting.

Data Information that is collected and manipulated within your computer program.

Deadline When the project must be completed. When placing advertising, a deadline is the absolute last opportunity to submit material.

Descender The part of a lowercase letter that goes below the baseline. Lowercase p, q, j, and are examples of descenders.

Dithered A way of creating colors and shades on a monitor by mixing pixels (dots) of different values. The adjacent pixels, when taken together, create the impression of a color. Dithering is done to give the impression of colors that aren't available for display.

Download To electronically recieve in one computer that which was sent by another computer.

DPI An acronym for dots per inch. A measure of resolution that expresses detail. (See RESOLUTION, page 122.)

Drop initial (See DISPLAY CAP, page 39.)

Dummy Another word for *mock-up*; a dummy is a preliminary layout that shows how a piece folds, etc. It is often useful to show a dummy to a printer if you are planning a complex job.

E-scale A convenient tool used for figuring out the size of type. An E-scale has a letter, usually the letter "E",

Continued

printed in several different sizes on clear plastic. You can match already-printed type to the letters printed on the scale in order to figure out its size.

Ellipses A series of three dots (....) Used to replace omitted copy.

Em-dash A long dash. An em-dash is the width of a capital letter "M."

EPS An acronym for Encapsulated PostScript. This is a file format that contains the PostScript instructions for constructing and printing a file. (See GRAPHIC, page 56, FILE FORMATS, page 47.)

Estimating A preliminary stage of a graphic design job where all costs — labor, materials, expenses etc. — are considered and accounted for, in order to determine the overall cost of a job. A professional graphic designer or desktop publisher always estimates a job and provides a client with a price before beginning a project.

Extended type The opposite of condensed. Extended type is wider than the normal letter width. Also called *expanded*.

Flyer A promotional hand-out. A flyer is usually one page.

Folio Another word for *page number*.

Foreground The area of a photograph or illustration that is towards front of the image.

Gradient Fill Another word for *blend*. (See BLEND, page 8.)

Grain When you look at a piece of paper, the fiber (particles of pulp) in the paper seems to run in a certain direction. This is the grain.

Grayscale Grayscale is the range of values (shades of gray) between black and white. The values between black and white are represented by varying densities of dots. Most devices — printers and monitors, for example, are capable of reproducing a fixed number of grays. Their grayscale might be 16 or more commonly 256. That means the device is capable of reproducing 256 shades of gray progressing from black to white.

Hairline   An extremly thin rule, approximately ¼ point (.25 pt.).

Heading   The bold line of type introducing or labeling the text that follows.

Illustration A picture. An illustration usually illuminates or supports the text in some way, or contains some kind of visual information. (See GRAPHIC, page 56.)

Imprint When you print information onto an already printed piece, as in the case of a business card that is printed with an employee's name after the rest of the card has been printed.

Initial Caps   Another word for *display caps*. (See DISPLAY CAPS, page 39.)

Jaggies The sharp-stepped edges of computer drawn type and graphics, an undesirable effect.

Kilobyte 1,024 bytes.

L.C. Short for *lowercase*.

Landscape   This refers to page that is set up horizontally.

Leader The row of characters that is used to connect tabbed material, as in a table of contents. (See DOT LEADER, page 44.)

Legal Refers to paper that is 8 ½" x 14" in size.

Legibility   Refers to the ease with which a particular typeface can be read. Legibility is inherent in the design of a typeface, unlike readability which is a combination of many factors.

Letter Refers to paper that is 8 ½" x 11". It is probably the most common size paper in daily use.

Letterhead Another word for a piece of stationery printed with a company or individual's name, address, and phone number and any other business information such as a logo.

Continued

229

Letterspacing Another word for *tracking*. (See TRACKING, pg. 168.)

Ligature Characters that have been joined and made available as a single character; the letters "ff" and "fl" are often included in a font as ligatures. This feature is more common in traditional typesetting than in desktop publishing, although many fonts include ligatures.

Line art Artwork made of solid lines and area of color. Line art does not have any gradual tones or blends.

Linespacing Another word for *leading*. (See LEADING, page 87.)

Lithography A common printing method. (See PRINTING, page 108.)

LPI Abbreviation for lines per inch, a measurement of halftone frequency. (See HALFTONE, page 66.)

Masthead The heading at the top of a newspaper or newsletter that regularly identifies the publication.

Megabyte One thousand kilobytes — usually abbreviated as M or MB.

Modem The device that sends digital data over telephone lines. You can use a modem to send files to a service bureau. (See SERVICE BUREAU, page 145.)

Non-repro blue A shade of light blue that is not reproducible by by copy machines, cameras, etc.

Oblique Type that slants to the right.

OCR An acronym for Optical Character Recognition. OCR software converts scanned pages of copy into a text format your computer can read.

Offset lithography A common and inexpensive printing method. (See PRINTING, page 108.)

Orientation The direction of a page in relation to a horizontal or vertical axis. A page that is oriented vertically is called *portrait*. A page that is oriented horizontally is called *landscape*.

Paste-up Another word for *mechanical*. (See MECHANICAL, page 97.)

Perforate A tiny row of small holes that allows paper — a coupon for example — to be easily torn.

Pica A unit of measure in typography. Six picas equal an inch.

Pixels Short for *picture elements*; these are the individual dots that make up an image. They usually refer to computer screens.

Point A small typographic unit of measure. There are 12 points in a pica.

Portrait This refers to a page that is set up vertically.

Posterize A special photographic effect that minimizes the number of shades of gray in a picture. (See SCAN-NING, page135.)

PostScript A computer language belonging to Adobe Systems Inc. that contains instructions for representing and describing type and images. (See FONT, page 51.)

Printer's error Usually notated as "PE." A printer's error is a mistake made by the typesetter (or computer operator), as opposed to an error or change made by the client.

Process printing Four color printing that reproduces full color images by using cyan, yellow, magenta and black ink. (See COLOR OFFSET PRINTING, page 28.)

Proof A version of a job in progress.

Pull quote Another word for *call out*.

Quote marks The double apostrophes that appear before and after a word or sentence to indicate that it is a quotation. There are two types of quote marks in desktop publishing: *curly quotes* and *neutered quotes*. Curly quotes (" ") curve either to the right or left, thus indicating whether the quote mark is opening or closing the quote. Neutered quote marks (" ") go straight up and down.

Ragged When type is not aligned, it is said to be *ragged*. For example, if type is flush left, it is ragged on the right. This means that the words that end at the right margin are not aligned.

Continued

GLOSSARY

Raw copy Copy that has not been formatted. (See COPY, page 33.)

Readability The degree to which type is easy to read. Readability is not based only on typeface selection; it is the sum of various qualities in a block of copy.

Ream 500 sheets of paper.

RGB Stands for red, green and blue, the color system used for display on a computer monitor.

Roman An upright and unitalicized letter.

Rough Another word for a *sketch*.

Sans serif Type that does not have serifs, the small strokes on the end of letters. (See SERIFS, page 142.)

Scoring The process where a piece of paper is prepared for folding. Heavy paper needs to be scored because otherwise the paper cracks or splits when folded.

Screen font A screen font is a bitmap rendering of a font designed to be displayed on a monitor.

Screen printing (See PRINTING, page 108.)

Sheet One piece of paper. Sheets come in many different sizes although most office printers can print on only a few of these sizes.

Spec Short for *specify*. In typesetting, you *spec type*, which means you select type sizes, typefaces, leading and other settings for your copy.

Spot color Refers to flat printing — printing done with pre-mixed color inks.

Spread Two pages that are side-by-side in a booklet or publication.

Stet A proofreaders' mark that means a correction should be ignored, and copy should be left as it was.

Stripping The stage in print preparation where photographic negatives (or positives) are assembled in position for printing.

Swash The long flourish that decorate certain ornamental typefaces. A swash usually extends from a capital letter.

Tabloid Refers to paper that is 11" x 17" in size. (See PAPER, page 106.)

Template A generic, ready-made piece of artwork that can be adapted to the user's individual need. Also known as a *boilerplate*.

Text Another word for *body copy*.

Text box A feature of some programs where text is placed in a box that can then be moved anywhere on the page.

TIFF Short for Tagged Image File Format. TIFF is a common file format used for representing graphics and photos.

Tiling A way of printing documents that are too large to print in one piece on a particular printing device. When you tile a document, you break it into smaller parts that can then be used to reconstruct a larger document.

Tint Another word for *shade*. In printing, a shade is most commonly referred to as a tint. (See SHADE, page 147.)

Transpose A proofreaders' term that indicates words, letters or sentences should be switched in position.

Trim To cut a piece of printed artwork down to its finished size.

Type All the symbols and characters that make up a printed language.

Typesetting The profession of preparing and assembling type for use reproduction. Professionally set type conforms to design principles as well as standards of readability. Type can be set by hand, machine, photo reproduction, and today, by microcomputer in the process of desktop publishing.

Typo An error made while typing.

Typography The art of creating and working with type. Typography has a history that dates back thousands of years. As in any art form, its practitioners look for originality, beauty and functionality in the creation of an alphabet.

Continued

GLOSSARY

U.P.C. An acronym for Universal Product Code. The series of vertical bars printed on most packages today, that contain digitized information about the product.

Vignette A picture whose edges are softened and fade to the background. Vignettes often give pictures a delicate, old-fashioned look.

Watermark The symbol or logo that is molded into paper. Better writing paper often comes with a watermark of the manufacturer. Some programs have a feature that lets users apply a mock watermark — a very light tint (shade) of a symbol or logo that appears on the page behind solid type.

Weight The variation in the apparent thickness of a typeface. There are many different weights from thin, ultra light, light, book, medium, regular, and text to bold, demi-bold, semi-bold, extra bold, ultra bold, heavy and black.

Window A method of display where a file in progress is displayed in a self contained window.

Word balloon The word-filled bubble that appears over the heads of characters in comics.

WYSIWYG Stands for What You See Is What You Get. This phrase refers to a type of computer display where the actual letterforms and graphics are rendered as they are meant to ultimately print.

Zoom To enlarge a picture on your computer screen (to zoom in), or to reduce a picture on your computer screen.

Index

Continued

INDEX

Continued

INDEX

FREE CATALOG
_&_
UPDATED LISTING

We don't just have books that find your answers faster; we also have books that teach you how to use your computer without the fairy tales and the gobbledygook.

We also have books to improve your typing, spelling and punctuation.

**Tear out the slip below and return it to us for a free catalog and mailing list update.**

RETURN TODAY!

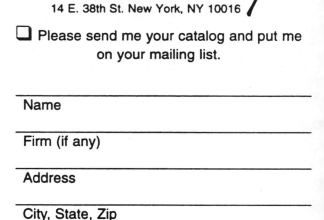

DDC *Publishing*

14 E. 38th St. New York, NY 10016

❑ Please send me your catalog and put me on your mailing list.

_____
Name

_____
Firm (if any)

_____
Address

_____
City, State, Zip